D1432361

PSYCHOTHEOLOGY

PSYCHOTHEOLOGY

by

E. Mark Stern

and

Bert G. Marino

PAULIST PRESS

Paramus / New York / Toronto

The authors wish to thank Eileen Jablonski, Janet Pertusi, Virginia Stern, and Joan Bel Geddes Ulanov for their help in the preparation of the manuscript, and Oona Sullivan for her invaluable suggestions as the book was being written.

Copyright ©1970 by
The Missionary Society
of St. Paul the Apostle
in the State of New York

Library of Congress
Catalog Card Number: 79-128142

ISBN 0-8091-1782-7

Published by Paulist Press
Editorial Office: 1865 Broadway, N.Y., N.Y.   10023
Business Office: Paramus, New Jersey   07652

Printed and bound in the
United States of America

CONTENTS

To
Robert Pollack
and
Marius Bewley

FOREWORD

After decades of viewing each other suspiciously as irreconcilables, religion and psychology have today come to the point of seeing each other as polar ends of a workable compromise. What religious counselor, for example, would presume to speak of sexual morality today without first acquainting himself with some of the insights that the study of human behavior can afford him? And what therapist can honestly ignore the meaning of religious training in forming the personality of the patient who says he is a professing Christian? In our time this uneasy truce has developed into a more meaningful relationship.

In an age when the sense of convergence is becoming more and more desired, unnecessary divisions are regarded with distaste. There is a level which, at least in the popular imagination, is the exclusive territory of neither religion nor psychology; rather, it is an offspring of the two with a unique identity of its own.

This book is not out to prove that a synthesis between theology and psychology is possible, but that in many respects it is already an accomplished fact. From a phenomenological point of view, spokesmen of both religion and psychology seem to be speaking in the same way about the same things, especially in such areas as guilt, sexual love, social conscience — just to cite a few obvious examples. The ordinary person today depends less on older dogmatic assertions no matter where they are to be found, and seeks answers which a single angle of vision affords. The approach taken in this book, which we have called "psychotheological," says that such an attitude is not only desirable but already a fact.

Of course, we will not be speaking of those difficulties that only a skilled psychotherapist can handle, but of those psychological, ethical, and social dilemmas that any person who wishes to deepen his moral sensitivity, for both spiritual and psychological reasons, can learn to handle with a minimum of skilled help and a maximum of honesty. Psychotheology claims that its emphasis on a single approach is justifiable because it assumes that there are many questions which experience itself can answer. This is not to imply that the "moral science" involved in religion and the "motivational science" we call clinical psychology are inadequate, but simply that many men today are instinctively turning to the wider category of their own experience where the two disciplines at times lose their self-imposed demarcations and become intermingled and mutually illuminating.

Henry James gave experience its most illuminating definition when he said in *The Art of Fiction:* "Experience is never limited, and it is never complete; it is an immense sensibility, a kind of huge spiderweb of the finest silken threads suspended in the chamber of consciousness, and catching every air-borne particle in its tissue. It is the very atmosphere of the mind . . . It takes to itself the faintest hints of life, it converts the very pulses of the air into revelations."

To some people the term psychotheology will convey a reasonably clear meaning. Yet some kind of working definition seems to be in order. First of all, this is an approach, as we have already said, which takes it for granted that men no longer believe that certain areas of their lives belong either to a religious or a psychological domain. By considering some vital questions from a single vantage point, we have the opportunity of drawing upon the insights of both religion and psychology without having to apologize for either. Experience has taught us that many of the great truths of our Judeo-Christian traditions — in the religious and the secular sense — are, before all else, great human truths, and commenting on them from a psychotheological viewpoint gives testimony to this fact.

The essays in this book almost always follow the same method. They often cluster psychological comment around some episode from the bible — one of the parables of Christ, for example, or one of the many stories in the Old Testament. *There are countless insights in the bible which have yet to be brought out and articulated in experiential psychological terms.* Such a method is by no means new. Ever since the dawn of Christianity, great minds of the Western world have sought to create a rapprochement between what in earlier days used to be referred to simply as the "revelations" of the Judeo-Christian religion and the inexpressible fascination they have had for the human mind. The great allegorists of the early centuries of Christianity — men like St. Augustine and Origen especially — constantly toyed with the idea that there was some kind of intimate correspondence between the mysteries of Christianity and the human heart. They were hard pressed, at times, for lack of a vocabulary, to pinpoint exactly where it lay; but at least they succeeded in initiating an approach which has never lost its appeal. With the triumph of Aristotelian rationalism, later centuries began to view this approach with suspicion to such an extent that it was eventually relegated to the level of the "mystical" or "poetic."

It was not until the 17th century, when the first great attempts were made to study the human mind as a phenomenon in itself, that the question of the difference between "supernatural" and "natural" truth was turned into a dilemma. Descartes' new epistemology finally revealed the question that Christianity had to face — whether the two levels of truth could ever be reconciled. It was inevitable, considering what Descartes had to say about the nature of the human mind as being self-sufficient and drawing its experience only from the natural world, that many people began to believe that the truths of "revealed religion" were available to the human mind only from "above." Descartes' great disciple, Spinoza, tried to bring the levels together, to such an extent that he was accused of pantheism. Later thinkers like Kant sought to explain the truths of the Christian moral experience by making them connatural to the mind itself. Everywhere — in philosophy and ethics — the attempt was made to bridge the dualism initiated by the Cartesian revolution.

By the dawn of the Freudian era, however, man's *soul* and man's *psyche* were sharply distinguished. So began the open conflict between religion and psychology, with both claiming that each held the "key" to the secret of human behavior and, more importantly, to human happiness. This tension was taken for granted until our own time. Psychology, with its therapeutic programs of psychiatry and psychoanalysis, began more and more to appropriate the role of arbiter of human affairs, convinced of the demise of religion as an important moral science.

Today we seem to be coming full circle, finding ourselves in a situation where such conflict is less and less acceptable. Our generation is demanding a more integrated approach to the problems of human life. Even with the great inroads psychology has made, much of its former authority is now being questioned. Even within the psychological "establishment," new lines of inquiry have begun under the encompassing headings of "humanistic psychology" and "existential psychotherapy." The main premise of both approaches states that man is as much involved in his search for meaning as he is with his native drives and perceptions. This development comes about not because the principles of the older psychologies are necessarily invalid, but because we have come to learn that the problems of life always shy away from one-dimensional solutions. More and more the younger generation especially is turning to the hope that involvement in life can tell them a great deal more than an easy trip to either the couch or the confessional.

The use of the term "psychotheological" to describe our approach may strike some as an anomaly. We are assuming, however, that there are many people who feel that the great ethical truths of Christianity, together with the modern psychological insights that illuminate them, can still tell us a great deal about human life. Other persons, of course, question this premise. Extreme secularists believe that such an approach is superfluous; traditional religionists will insist that it is a reckless venture into rationalizing and even downgrading the "transcendent" truths of Christianity whose eternal values can never use experience for confirmation. Although both groups may find it difficult to agree with the general approach of this book, both are nevertheless saying the same thing: Christianity has little to tell us about man in the here-and-now.

In a sense, it is the believing Christian who might have the greater difficulty appreciating what the psychotheological approach attempts to do. This is perhaps because catechizing and sermonizing, at least until recently, was pretty much given over to exploring the New Testament in order to justify the claims of Christianity as a divinely instituted religion. To search out the scriptures for anything more than that may appear to such people as a hopeless task. What they are really saying is that the parables and even those mysterious events of Christ's life which still defy rational analysis show that Christianity is basically an "other-worldly" religion and had better be left at that.

Rousseau, whose brand of Christianity has never been easy to define, characterized this attitude aptly and wittily when he said that the trouble with Christianity was that it was not interested in forming a society of man but a society of angels. We, of course, have taken exactly the opposite position, for we believe that an examination of the teachings of Christ — even an analysis (as far as it can go) of some of his miracles — reveals psychodynamic principles of inestimable importance for the human condition.

Some people, who don't share Rousseau's somewhat cynical nostalgia of what Christianity *could* be, believe Christianity is no longer of any value to a modern generation even for the moral sanctions that it affords. They charge religion with having allowed itself to be used as a way of ignoring life and the reality of everyday anxieties. It is certainly true that the "angelistic" approach is always the temptation of religion when it sets its sights on another world. There can be no question here of the great challenge that psychology has thrown in the path of Christianity; it has every right to complain that there is a dehumanizing tendency at work in religion. But even the staunchest humanists will at least have to allow for the fact that this attitude is not necessarily founded on any defect in Christianity when it is used by believers as a genuine life-style, as opposed to how Freud described it — an illusory escape.

But making an apology for Christianity is not our immediate purpose. We do want to demonstrate that many of the insights derived from psychotherapeutic psychology can help us cull certain perceptions from the New Testament which bear upon experience and life itself. Certainly no one can deny that our approach is at least experimentally valid.

For example, in dealing with the question of conscience, we try to show how man's morally conscious life can expand only to the degree that it reacts to certain life situations where it becomes increasingly aware of its own freedom in making value judgments. As a starting point we use the legend of the Garden of Eden, which was an attempt to come to grips with a human but nonetheless mysterious phenomenon. By using a psychological approach as well as a religious one, we hope to face the objections that will arise in a psychological frame of reference. On this issue, psychotherapeutic psychology has been quick to insist that to show that conscience exists is not enough, that it poses for many men greater problems than it solves. In other words, by examining human motivation one is forced to question the sometimes narrow character that religion has assigned to the power of moral judgment. Psychoanalytic psychology does this by revealing the ambiguity and the ambivalence of much of our moral activity. But psychotheology steps in at this point and shows that Christ himself, in the famous parable of the wheat and the weeds, gave testimony to the existence of such ambivalence long before it was psychologically articulated. Indeed, we find time and time again that Christ, who often speaks in simple terms of virtue and vice, frequently demonstrates that he did not have a simplistic approach to life, as many think. He is the first to remind us, for example, in the parable just mentioned, that an immature understanding of one's moral power can have disastrous results. (And who better than Christ came to know the evil of moral narrowness?) In many instances, Christ, in simple but lofty language, gave moral safeguards which only now we have come to appreciate as powerful psychological weapons. The fact that such subtlety is to be found in the New Testament may astonish some persons; but the more astonishing fact is that we could have been reading it all these years and overlooking so many of the subtler characteristics of Christ's thought. We have tended to emphasize the "lofty" (too often a euphemism for "simplistic") aspects of what he said. We have turned his challenges to human moral behavior into moral imperatives of our own making.

Psychology, unwittingly or not, has forced Christianity into areas where each must confront the other not as enemies, nor even as allies, but as brothers. The emergence of the field of pastoral counseling, which gives trained clergymen healing skills from both psychology and the spiritual tradition, is one example of this union. There are, of course, other areas where such an ideal union is still impossible; but those instances may indicate not so much an impossible deadlock as they do a yet-to-be-discovered level of mutual illumination, where certain aspects of human experience have yet to be approached from an integrated angle of vision.

In the essays which comprise this book, we have limited ourselves to those areas where Christianity and psychology are indeed speaking in the same voice. There are times when psychology, especially when dealing with human motivation, seems to speak more clearly; but there are other instances where human motivation is shrouded in mystery, where the human soul seems to expose itself only under the magnetism of religious inspiration. Those are the moments when, as William James has put it, "faith as a fact can help create a fact." Many of Christ's words seem to use this technique: An ethical imperative is stated without proof or explanation — as, for example, in the case of the Beatitudes — and it is only in the free acceptance of it for its sheer moral power that we are led in turn to an investigation of why it attracted us in the first place. Eventually, even the hidden psychodynamic principles Christ is using, but did not explicitly state, often become, with the help of psychological insight, abundantly clear.

We live in an ecumenical age. The desire for moral ecumenism far outstrips in importance even the hoped for, eventual reunion of the churches of Christendom. A common moral ground, a sense of the worldwide strength of moral force, seems to be growing with each generation. Psychotheology looks to religion and psychology as sources of nourishment for such a force.

The ineluctable laws of life and love govern both the soul and psyche of men, for these are different names for the single power we call his *heart*. There, at least, men of truth and honesty know there can be no division.

1

HUMAN FREEDOM
AND DEVELOPMENT

From the viewpoint of psychotheological inquiry, the apparent dichotomy between the religious emphasis on transcendence and psychology's insistence on the importance of the here-and-now is not as crucial as it first appears to be. Experience reassures us that most men can work and live comfortably with such a polarity. Every person desires both autonomy and the yearning for union with more than himself. Changes or growth would be impossible without a constant shift from self-concern to an increasing awareness of one's relationship to the rest of reality.

Freedom

The biblical account of the Garden of Eden poses this problem in a myth. Within the confines of the protected Garden, man had everything he needed. His need for a mate was fulfilled even before he asked. But then he reached out for something more. He felt the need for a deeper kind of fulfillment. Religion has traditionally described this — the desire for autonomy — as the original moral rebellion, perhaps to account for what experience itself confirms time and again: that, historically, man's desire for autonomy too often has been a mask for selfishness, injustice and

9

even murder. But religion has also tended to accept the prejudice that every autonomous desire is in some way a reminder of man's original act of defiance.

Adam's "original" sin is not called original merely because it was the first, but because it is seen as the root of everything that is wrong with man. To explain evil this way has given man's religious instinct a convenient way of describing and handling the moral chaos he experiences every day of his life. Yet it is experience itself that tells us that the desire for selfhood — even at the risk of "losing" God — is a basic instinct. How can any man escape his own isolation, how can he be born psychologically, unless he experiences the power of his own will?

Life in the womb, we are tempted to believe, is all idyllic harmony. But in addition to being a time of pre-conscious development, it is also a preparation for something beyond itself. The womb, like the Garden, is a shelter. The little we know of the evolution of man as a conscious being tells us that he always sees situations like this as potential traps. If the legend of Eden has anything meaningful to say in psychotheological terms, it must confirm what we know from experience: that no one wants to remain in a state of absolute predictability.

Christianity has traditionally interpreted man's movement out of his perfect surroundings as a catastrophe. The most psychotheology can say is that any step forward into consciousness, even when it seems to be moral revolt, can never be *per se* destructive.

Christianity has also seen the Eden sin as a blessing, and on this level it takes on a much deeper psychological significance. The doctrine of the "fortunate fall" so celebrated in the history of Christianity and art is an attempt to make some psychological sense out of the simplistic narrative of the bible. "O happy fault, that merited us so great a Redeemer!" cries the ritual on Holy Saturday night. Psychotheology goes further: Man's fall was not merely a fortunate accident; it was, in a psychological sense, his birthright. Every man's freedom involves risk. The fact that man falls from his ideals is not simply a result of his exercise of freedom; it is rather a misadventure in the direction of whatever goals he has set for himself. The need for risk is both an experiential fact and a sacred obligation. Risk puts one in jeopardy, but is the only means of progress and engagement. Christian thinkers have frequently wondered whether it would have been better if man had never risked losing his original idyllic life. Experience answers that risk is the stuff out of which autonomy is made. Speculation about the beauty of primitive "pre-lapsarian" existence is fruitless and frustrating. If the biblical account of Eden is read with any kind of insight, it is obvious that man knew from the beginning that without risk he was doomed to a life not of innocence but of infantilism.

The Eden experience does indeed reflect what life alone can tell us about man: He cannot live without the possibility of failure. The prohibition of the Lord in the Garden was not so much an absolute injunction as it was a forewarning of the dangers inherent in any act of emancipation. While the command not to eat the fruit did not deal with responsibility in the most mature sense, it was a warning of what responsibility entails. The difference between bounden duty and the capacity for moral decision is to be found only in man's willingness to fail on his own terms. Viewed positively, God's warning was not restrictive; it was the opportunity for expansion through the assertion of personal authenticity.

Man's first intimation of autonomy comes at the moment of separation from his mother's body, with the shock of consciousness that proclaims his selfhood. He takes a breath and becomes aware of his ability to experience, to live. For his first few months in his mother's arms he continues to live in an autistic world. He cannot discriminate between himself and his surroundings. His mother, the walls, the crib, are one Eden. The psychoanalytic theorist would say that the infant is in no position to recognize object relationships. He is in a symbiotic, or completely identified, position with his mother. But even this Eden cannot persist for any length of time. He wants more of what experience can afford him. He first learns this unwittingly through a sense of isolation when he discovers that not everything is at his beck and call. He cries when the extension of himself called "Mother" does not immediately appear. His cries may be what we later call prayer, and as the world of experience widens, so too does his level of prayer

expand by his learning to trust. Erik Erikson has pointed out that
trust is the first "developmental task" of the infant. Only as the
lesson is learned is the infant in any position to ratify his sense
that he is part of a larger world. It is no accident that the first
game played with little children in many cultures is some variation
of "peek-a-boo" where the psychological separation from another
has a chance to happen in a trusting atmosphere. Through the
appearance and reappearance of the mother (or some other
significant adult) the first fruits of trust are born. Experience,
instinct — call it what you will — tells us this lesson in autonomy
is the first step in the developmental pattern of the upbringing of
the infant.

The story of Eden is a way of explaining why man, as he continues throughout life to experience infantilism, should resist the
temptation to capitulate and be overdependent upon God. Even
the consequent real possibility of alienation from his Creator does
not deter him from preserving his autonomy at all costs. But it
also reminds us of the far more important psychotheological
principle: that often we turn from God in order to find him again
in a more meaningful way. The degree of panic and anxiety we as
adults continue to feel in moments of religious frustration may very
well be traced to early experiences of separation when as infants
we were not given the opportunity to learn to trust. The adult too
often interprets his unhappy moments of pain and isolation as
God's "desertion."

Moments of separation or loss are opportunities for building
faith in oneself. Just as in Eden, man eventually comes to risk
being alone. The infant in his periods of aloneness has to face the
opportunity of becoming either hysterical or productive. If he opts
for the latter it is because he discovers dimensions of himself —
even if only through his toes, or through the aromas, sounds and
colors around him, or the fascination for his own sounds. This
encounter with the self, this experiment in locating the shifting
tides of one's personality, creates the rationale of self-appreciation.

By asserting one's autonomy, the way is prepared for eventual
union with the world and the formation of real relationships. We

can say — and it is just as true for us now — that in the legend of the first man and woman rebellion did not necessarily indicate total disavowal. The need for union with the Creator continued, just as an infant continues to need its mother for physical sustenance and emotional protection. By asserting his autonomy a person can discover the need to be joined with someone or something other than himself. It can put him in a more authentic relationship to the world, and to the power we call God.

Love may be all that religion says it is. But before all else, it is a power which bridges the gap between man's sense of separateness and his desire to join with others. The infant who learns to separate himself from his mother seeks a greater social identity. His next steps are in the direction of unity with his family and his friends so that he is in a position to participate in some kind of union that transcends himself, so that he has the opportunity to grow.

As adults, our misgivings about relationships with others often seem to stem from some long forgotten fear of infantile desertion. Our jealousy, our emotional clinging to others, are all types of peace maneuverings, attempts to protect ourselves from what we consider an unfriendly environment. Child therapy has shown that with children who have had such fears, a first step is made by stressing a trustful environment, so the child might learn that separation does not keep him forever at odds with his environment.

Man's assertion of autonomy establishes his sense of values, and it also introduces him to the reality of conflict. The consequence of the original rebellion, "the knowledge of good and evil" — of virtue and sin — may be, psychotheologically speaking, alternating forces which perpetually adjust the shifting strands of conscious deliberation. Humans are constantly seeking to systematize new experiences in order to put them into workable order. It is only when our morality becomes a rigid construct of laws, an ossification of experiences, that we obscure, in the name of morality, the necessity (not merely the inevitability) of the conflict necessary for growth. The frustrations we encounter are very often self-imposed and spring from notions of what we think our behavior should be. But history, beginning with the legend of the Garden, has shown that man will fight for and protect his autonomy, even if it means he has to endure conflict.

Psychotheological insight warns against rigid ethical strangle-holds which stifle rather than foster conflict. A person who accepts the value of moral sensitivity but who uses psychology to keep his motives and spirit hygienically clean is always able to keep his sense of balance. Sometimes what goes by the name of religion is really a refusal to believe that man can live without the crutch of traditions, without the need to turn back or revert to dead idols. Religion often makes public testimony of the importance of new-ness without the full psychological appreciation of what it means. For instance, the resurrection of Christ from the dead has been accepted by many as an historical fact, but it is less often stressed as an available experience. Men are always looking for a revision and revitalization of life expressions. It is only the fearful who discourage revision as a sign of weakness and instability.

Psychotheology celebrates restlessness as a sacrament, as a sign that everyone's exercise of autonomy is essential for growth. The ultimate goal in Western culture often seems to rest in a constant need for self-contentment. A religious attitude not pro-tected by psychological safeguard created our lifeless notion of heaven when it promises that man's "rebellious will" finally will be "soothed" by love. It would be truer to suppose that heaven is a place where we have reached full autonomy, but only because we have reached the point where we can appreciate what life has had to offer.

Development

The story Genesis recounts is an important prototypical attempt to describe the mysterious beginnings of human freedom. Its less obvious implication can be brought into sharper focus by a free use of what psychology has to say about human motivation. The important thing to stress, however, from a psychotheological view-point is that the experience of which both religion and psychology speak is essentially the same.

Man's maturity always depends on what he does with his free-dom. Any growth implies change, but psychospiritual growth makes sense only in terms of what new levels of consciousness he feels compelled to aim for. There is inherent in any judgment of ethical and psychological importance a sense of what we can call psychospiritual teleology, or purposefulness.

It was the central insight of the great French evolutionist Teil-hard de Chardin that the concepts of evolution and convergence are intimately linked. There are those, of course, who disagree with this association, who maintain that evolutionary laws operate without any necessary reference to teleological outlook. But psy-chotheology believes that man's religious and psychological yearn-ings are constantly converging and interacting for an end.

Psychotheology accepts the reality of convergent activity, for it believes that we are living in a world which is becoming, not merely a world that is. As part of the unfolding evolution of the universe, man grows by constantly reaching out for transpersonal union: not only for a society or even a God he thinks he knows, but for those he has yet to discover.

Extreme humanists may arch their brows at the suggestion that purposefulness has a real role to play in evolution. Teleology does not carry much weight today, especially in scientific circles. Con-versely, religious orthodoxy has always limited its notions of teleology to a purely abstract level. It believes that teleology has little to do with man except to furnish him with arguments proving the existence of a designer of the universe, and that it has had little connection with the notion of man's spiritual and moral evolution. On a theological level, Christianity has resisted the idea that evolution touches, in an analogical fashion, every level of reality, including man's unfolding relationship to God and his fellow man. But neither secular humanism nor abstract theology has said the final word on this point.

From the beginning of the Darwinian revolution, theologians were fearful that Darwin's theories would rob man of his "primacy" as the one being with a soul given directly by God. But although Darwin's theories are now seen less and less as a threat to a spiritual definition of man, religion has still not openly acknowledged the full implications of evolutionary theory. In his 1952 encyclical *Humani Generis,* for example, Pope Pius XII stated that "the teaching of the Church leaves the doctrine of evolution as an open question — as long as it confines its speculations to the development of the human body." But in point of fact evolution has a great deal to tell us — if not of the creation of the soul, then certainly of the phenomenological aspects of man's growth and change. The distinction people make between "soul" and "psyche" is at best semantic cowardice, and in a psychotheological context is purely arbitrary. When we wish to safeguard the unchanging nature of man's spiritual nature — his immortality, his rationality — we speak of his "soul"; when we speak of man's more baffling characteristics — his irrationality and unpredictability — we refer to his "psyche." The fact is, of course, that it is one psychospiritual power that undergoes change.

Studies in comparative religion and religious anthropology have made this abundantly clear. Darwin said that the struggle for existence between tribes depended upon moral and intellectual sophistication. He theorized that only a group ready to make sacrifices for the common good could hope to survive. Man's spiritual and moral evolution can be seen only in terms of his increasing psychosocial awareness. Indeed, in our time, the theme of the "extended tribe" as embracing the entire human race is itself becoming necessary for survival.

In spite of the difficulties traditional Christianity has had in speaking of the human personality in psychodynamic terms, it is enlightening and remarkable to discover how often in the New Testament Christ does not hesitate to do so, especially in those instances where he deals with the human personality on a level which makes no real distinction between man's religious and psychological drives. The full psychotheological range of the New Testament regarding the nature of the human personality must be left to later chapters, but for now even a cursory glance at some of Christ's teachings reveals certain insights of inestimable value for religion *and* psychology.

Christ speaks clearly of man's radical capacity for change. He does not equate men's tendency to resist this innate capacity simply in terms of man's "sinful nature." He speaks of it as a blindness which flows from man's inability to see his own radical capacity for higher levels of consciousness. Christ says: "Unless a man is born through water and the Spirit he cannot enter the Kingdom of God" (John 3, 5), and thus he exhorts man in religious terms to accept the truth about the dynamism of the human personality.

In a psychotheological context, one does not have to limit these famous words to the traditional Christian insistence upon the necessity of baptism. Even that immemorial ritual is, after all, an external commemoration of the belief that man is capable of changes of which even he is not immediately aware.

"What is born of the flesh is flesh; what is born of the Spirit is spirit," Christ continues in the same passage. The distinction made between physical and spiritual birth does not necessarily refer to a dichotomy between flesh and spirit. In psychotheological terms, Christ is viewing man's birth on both levels as a *single experience.* The analogy suggests that birth on a spiritual level can be appreciated only in light of the experience that each man has already had in time. More importantly, Christ sees them as two moments in man's single journey. That journey from its first moments in the mysterious darkness of the womb begins with a pre-conscious acceptance of the ability for incredible expansion and radical change.

Even more can be said by using an evolutionary theory which sees the "root experience" in teleological terms. Natural birth becomes more meaningful in terms of what future births man is destined for. Physical birth is thus a first moment in all that is to follow. "Lower" experiences (those which are antecedent in time) are seen in terms of the "higher" experiences they prepare man for. The lower makes final sense in terms of the higher, not vice versa.

Christ does not stop here. He often speaks of man's continual resistance to growth and involvement. Man insists upon creating discords from which he finds it difficult to extricate himself. In the New Testament, Christ offers a simple but ingenious description of this phenomenon:

"Imagine a sower going out to sow. As he sowed, some seeds fell on the edge of the path, and the birds came and ate them up.

Others fell on patches of rock where they found little soil and sprang up straight away, because there was no depth of earth; but as soon as the sun came up they were scorched and, not having any roots, they withered away. Others fell among thorns, and the thorns grew up and choked them. Others fell on rich soil and produced their crop, some a hundredfold, some sixty, some thirty. Listen, anyone who has ears" (Matthew 13, 4-9).

The situation Christ enumerates here can be seen as a description of the different psychological reactions to his environment that man experiences. The fruitlessness of the first three levels is expressed in a sense of discord between the seed and its environment; but the last stage is the most meaningful because there the seed and the soil have interacted fully. Growth reached development on the level where a man achieved full union with his environment. He matured morally and psychologically only because he did not view experience as hostile.

The fact that man, through a series of resistances, can come to a deeper sense of union is a way of saying that without a sense of moral purposiveness the evolutionary impulse in itself will always remain blind. Each choice man makes as he grows can put him at odds with the world or lead him to greater cooperation with all that life has to offer. Evolutionary laws are not bound by man's desire to seek fulfillment on his own terms. Evolutionary progress does find fulfillment in the convergence that Teilhard speaks of, but not without the sense of purpose that man alone can give it.

Man is always on the brink of chaos. He is free to reject the therapeutic power of history, to return to barbarism, and he is free to choose what will be productive in the future. As he grows psychologically more sophisticated, his notions of good and evil become more subtle. There is as much reason for him to despair as to hope. Evolution has had little to tell man about how to handle this constant tendency to despair. True, the seed which we were, the growth which we continue to experience as we reach out for union with life and other men, indicate that man is potentially an expression of all creation. But the only kind of optimism that will really serve is one which is born of religious idealism and psychological honesty. The Christian tradition has always believed in a millennium, the "hundredfold" return of which Christ speaks in the parable. But Christ in this very parable warns man to temper his moral optimism with psychological truth. Even the most sacred goals are out of reach without this balance.

If we accept discord as a phenomenological fact and not merely as a metaphysical dilemma, we are better prepared to handle the anxiety that continues to plague us. To confuse cosmic optimism with romanticism is to pose more dilemmas than solutions. Men who live in a world of impending nuclear destruction and race riots are not so easily convinced that the human race is destined for an exclusively glorious future.

The study of human motivation that we call psychology has done a great deal to illuminate and assuage this anxiety. But no amount of rationalization can help man find the goals that his religious instincts tell him to reach for. A sophisticated psychological vocabulary means nothing without taking cognizance of the powerful reality of moral idealism. Before the advent of clinical psychology, the anxiety or sense of discord in life was seen exclusively in terms of sin. As man grew more enlightened, it was attributed to human "ignorance." But neither traditional Christianity nor modern psychological sophistication has offered a complete explanation for discord or what its purpose is in the evolutionary scheme of things. Yet together they offer hope that men can come to grips with discord in human life.

The discord Christ describes in the parable above can be seen as a moment in man's evolutionary journey; by no stretch of the imagination is it desirable for its own sake. Even Eastern religious practice has regarded discord as a basic evil. It has emphasized the ideal of an unresisting style of life where the ultimate goal is to bring mind and environment into a single whole. "He who is at harmony," the Bhagavad-Gita says, "gives up the fruit of his actions and thereby attains abiding Peace, whereas he who is not at harmony is attached to the fruit of his actions by desire and is in a state of bondage" (IV, 19, 20).

Western man has never proposed such a static view of reality as a real answer to discord. The anxieties and polarities of life, he believes, have an inescapable reality. The distinction which Christianity has insisted upon in the past between "supernatural" and "natural" confirms this fact in the sense that it recognizes the reality of the difference (and even the conflict) between man and his transcendent goals. Too often, of course, Christianity has pitted man against his environment in the guise of protecting his sense of the transcendent being we call God. But the inherent dualism that has characterized Western religion has also kept man on the horns of a fruitful psychological dilemma and forced him into what seems like the contradictory role of both accepting and rejecting the value of human experience. The love for and distrust of experience has led him more deeply into a never-ending search for higher platforms of understanding, for a deeper knowledge of God and man on grounds more compatible with his growing sense of involvement. This is precisely where the psychological revolution has been most important. Like technological advancement, it has helped man change his environment so as to achieve a deeper communion with it.

The changes effected in man's interior world are just as important as anything science has achieved. When Freud, for example, saw in the Oedipus struggle an indication of the everlasting tendency of man's attempts to relocate his faith in others, he furnished man with a new psychological environment for working out his relationship to God. The fact that Freud's purpose was to prove that the fatherhood of God was an illusory phase of the psychological struggle between parent and child need not concern us here. For on the psychotheological level the dynamism of his principle throws a great deal of light on how and why modern man has *de facto* discarded his earlier notion of God.

The "death of God" theory, in psychotheological terms, can be described as a struggle to attain a more mature relationship with God. Man had to outgrow his earlier need for magic and incantations to a God who was thought to hold rigid control over natural forces. As he comes to feel more and more control over those forces himself, he no longer believes in a God who strictly controls the universe. In this sense the "atheism" we hear so much of today is merely a negation of an outworn phase of mental and spiritual environment, and thus can be seen as a phase of faith itself.

When Christ speaks of the seed which fell on good soil and produced its fruit a hundredfold, he is describing that type of personality which has entrusted its religious and psychological instincts to the therapy that only experience and life can give. Life is a universal arena where the simple moral demands of Christ can be carried out regardless of creed or color or nationality. "You must love your God with all your heart, with all your soul, and with all your mind. This is the greatest and first commandment . . . The second resembles it: You must love your neighbor as yourself" (Matthew 22, 37-40). The difficulty man experiences in his attempts to fulfill these injunctions can only be explained in terms of his failure to see them as ethical imperatives of life, not merely as suggestions.

But as man's definition of God changes, so does his moral behavior. As he grows more keenly aware of the interplay between personality and environment, he becomes less apt to feel the need for a codified morality imposed from without by other men. Thus, as men become more psychologically attuned to each other's needs in the common bond of experience, they become freer to synthesize a more universal — and, to that extent, more secure — moral sense.

An inquisitional mind can never permit the existence of such an attitude because it insists that it alone has total moral vision. Traditionally, organized religions have appropriated this role to themselves. Psychotheology would say that they are not free to do this if it impairs the human psychological drive toward moral unity and harmony. Experience reveals that moral arrogance, wherever found, far from integrating mankind's moral sense, succeeds only in fragmenting it.

The life of the past need not govern the life of the future. The growth of universal moral force is a hope of the 20th century. There is a feeling today that humanity will someday come together on a level that we still can't comprehend. And for all the changes that our personalities will have to undergo, we know that there is a psychospiritual imperative to love.

The petals of man's expanding morality unfold slowly and only as men confront experience on the level where they see psychological drives and moral yearning as one. If the mysteries of this relationship are not completely understood at this point in our evolutionary journey, there are at least certain fundamental psychospiritual levels where such a convergence is not impossible or unreal.

The Jesus of the New Testament offers the possibility of such unity. His was a life where every polarity, even the human and the divine, was in a constant state of convergence. From a psychotheological viewpoint, the human personality is constantly striving to integrate moral and emotional drives in order to unite all men in the common quest for a deeper union with God. Christ's words in this regard are a hallmark: "May they be one in us," he prayed to the Father, "as you are in me and I in you" (John 17, 21).

2

SIN

The last chapter ended on a note of hope. The evolution of human consciousness goes hand in hand with the promise of moral convergence which can bring unity to man, individually and collectively. But the great call of Christ to unity, although accepted rationally by Western civilization, remains largely unheeded. The unity Christ envisioned has not yet found a complete response in the hearts of men or in the institutions men have created. How then can it be shown that this goal is the fulfillment of man's moral and psychological aspirations? How can experience speak to all men in the same way?

Moral Conflict

Psychology, for its own reasons, has offered many theories concerning man's continuing resistance to the goal of unity. It has gone a long way in accounting for the confusion and frustration that continue to riddle human activity. Although motivational psychology is still in its infancy as a science, experience does confirm what psychology has thus far emphasized — that man's volitional life, for reasons we do not yet fully understand, continues to be full of emotional and moral confusion.

Psychological observations on the confusion of much of man's behavior have, at least traditionally, been accepted only with reluctance by Christian moralists. They see an adequate explanation

23

for discord in man's tendency to sin, which they assert is the result of moral perversion and a distortion of values. Psychologists, to the extent that they deal with sin at all, reject the moralists' view as long as it implies that a man who wishes to be moral will be so, simply with the "grace of God."

A dynamic approach such as psychotheology which respects moral and psychic aspiration must begin by agreeing with psychology, at least to the extent that any religious exhortation to moral reform must, in order to have any value at all, be based upon the facts of experience.

Both psychology and religion speak of the conflicts in human behavior as if they were speaking of two separate activities. Indeed, the suspicion between religion and psychology is greatest when each tries to explain the reasons for conflict. Religion says that what psychology often excuses as "confusion" is explained by man's innate proclivity to evil, and that even the subtlest psychological vocabulary cannot diminish this truth. Psychology counters that what religion is quick to call "sinful behavior" is invariably the result of immaturity. Describing evil as the result of an "original sin" or as "privation of the good" does not seem to tell us much. Moreover, as psychologists point out, those who profess a deep belief in the grace of God are not thereby immune to conflictual or immoral behavior.

Even when stated in such simple terms, this argument is largely one of semantics. It is always easy to mistake labels for solutions. The distinction between religion's "virtue" and "sin" or psychology's "constructive and destructive behavior" seems unimportant when one faces the fact that moral discord is as much a reality today as it ever was, and that men persist in misbehaving despite all sanctions — whether based on the fear of hellfire or the more sophisticated threat of emotional anxiety. Before evil can be faced as reality, one must discover what it is that makes it at one and the same time morally and psychologically reprehensible.

If psychology and religion remain at loggerheads over the question, it is principally because psychology insists that easy moralizing is not a solution to anything. Psychology seeks to create a climate conducive to human change, not one that favors static solutions. The psychological attitude has never been particularly amenable to those moralists who judge human behavior in terms of ineluctable moral laws. This moral "legalism," although not as powerful today as it once was, has nevertheless been a major factor in the continuing alienation between religion and psychology. But the time has come to seek the moral rejuvenation of mankind by the creation of a synthesis between the laws of psychology and religion, laws which heretofore were thought to have little in common.

A Psychotheological Definition of Sin

We saw in the first chapter how the first man and woman may have been more obedient than they realized when they followed their impulse to be free. Rebellion is not in itself always evil. Testing new rules invariably involves breaking old ones. The desire to experience the new is deep in all men, no matter how psychologically enigmatic or morally dangerous it might seem.

Christ himself had to break many traditional patterns of his religious culture. He refused to bow to tradition for its own sake. Pious rationalizing has insisted that "rebellion" was excusable in his case because he was "divinely motivated." But this does not diminish the fact that it was rebellion, and as such necessary for the fulfillment of his own unique religious mission.

The accusation that religion has often made against psychology — that it tacitly fosters moral anarchy — becomes irrelevant when one considers that rebellion for its own sake has never had any special role to play in the economy of the psyche. Experience shows how rebellion can lead to anarchy as well as progress. But the psychological insight is clear and unwavering: The dynamic components of man's independence are his only means of keeping his sense of freedom alive. A moral climate cannot exist when man is deprived of his right to give shape to the raw material of experience.

We have a good case in point of how limited the traditional definition of sin is when we consider modern racism. Here even a person who thinks he is in tune with the fundamental laws of morality can connive at social immorality and in the process feel no sense of being rebellious or at odds with the laws of nature or of nature's God. Indeed, religion has had little to say, except in a general rhetorical way, about the sacredness of human brotherhood precisely because it has not clearly seen the commandment of brotherly love as a psychodynamic law intrinsic to human behavior. Moreover, religion becomes a perpetrator of immorality when it tacitly restricts its definition of morality and allows the laws of human brotherhood to be flaunted with impunity. By psychotheological standards this kind of thinking is as immoral as any overt "rebellion" against a commandment, since it operates on the principle that virtue has little to do with maturity, that man is capable of morality quite apart from a sense of social values.

It has been simple for a Christianity allied with middle-class concepts of morality to permit a man's sense of community to shrink until it includes no one but himself, his wife and his children — all of whom he sees as extensions of himself. For many this can be done without the slightest sense of rebellion against any law, human or divine. "Morality" of this kind is always fraudulent because it ignores, deliberately or not, man's psychospiritual need for moral convergence. Love for neighbor — be he black or yellow, living next door or thousands of miles away — can easily become a matter of supererogation, relegated to the level of moral fantasy or wish-fulfillment. Experience itself sets the limit for what both religion and psychology can honestly say about the nature of immorality — that it can never be viewed simply in terms of individual needs. The only meaningful morality, as psychotheology views it, is motivated by the need to generate mature, loving relationships between persons. Modern religion, especially when it exists in a democratic environment, defends the notion of personal rights but too often in the narrowest sense. It must share the blame for the fact that justice for many men is limited to a world so small that it includes no obligation except to those in one's immediate circle.

An attitude tainted by a narrow religious and political bias (and in America it is often hard to distinguish between the two) cannot do much to help a man evolve a deeper sense of morality. A morality so biased is inoperative because it is almost totally lacking in psychological depth. A man may say that he knows what he *wants* without having any notion of what he *needs*. The right to "life, liberty and the pursuit of happiness" becomes a euphemism when one believes that morality is limited to personal immediate needs. The belief that we must do everything for and by ourselves is immorality in the truest sense, for it presumes that we can function without others. There are those who still may view immorality abstractly as "rebellion" against the laws of God. More often than not, the psychic disturbance we call "rebellion" against God's laws is a direct result of the more basic immorality of self-isolation, when a man's sense of being trapped by his own limitations will lead him to outrage, hatred and violence.

The fact that men are free to mold experience to their selfish "needs" does not mean that experience will always yield what they wish it to yield. Psychology is right in insisting that men must grow beyond a yearning for complete security. Psychotheology suggests further than man's response to the ideals of generosity and selflessness is the only way he can give depth to experience.

This idea would be pure fantasy except for the fact that moral teleology has had a profound influence in the history of mankind, even if one views ethical idealism only in purely historical terms. Any student of American history knows, for example, to what extent the American dream was predicated upon moral drive, and this in a land which in the beginning had little to offer by way of material security.

Immorality is always rooted in psychospiritual infantilism. A baby, in his desire to acquaint himself with the world, tries to put everything into his mouth. For adults this takes the form of trying to seize whatever seems satisfying, regardless of what it may cost in retarding their own personal growth or in hindering that of others. The overbearing father, for example, feels secure only when he can manipulate his family according to his own needs. His idea of parental protectiveness is to keep a tight rein on his children, pushing them along on what he conceives to be the only path of moral behavior. Far from being moral, this attitude is simply infantilism rooted in a sense of moral arrogance.

By willfully clinging to moral isolation, a person smothers his imagination and weakens his relation to experience and the people who are part of it, principally because it generates a constant search for personal security. Our moral faculty becomes more and more limited to the narrow world of our own existence, whether that of family, country or church.

According to psychotheology, then, actions can properly be called sinful only when they cut men off from experience and encourage them in the fantasy that they can operate alone. Immorality in this sense is more than an individual act of rebellion. It is a force that can quietly poison the life of any moral system, even the most well-intentioned.

Moral Ambivalence

Ambivalence is an important factor of human behavior. Emotional health is never simply a matter of choosing between clear alternatives. For Freud the individual is caught between opposing forces of the *id,* the seat of all aggression (mostly sexual in nature), and the *super-ego,* the center of all social sanctions. Reconciliation between them takes place in the *ego.* Jung saw the *id* as more than the seat of libidinous forces. To him it also encompassed the collective unconscious history of the human race. In either case, both theories — as "abstract" as any religion has to offer — contend that what a man does is a combination of what he does and does not understand.

Thus in the long run neither the moralist nor the psychologist can claim the final word in explaining man's volitional activity. Only together can they furnish us with some understanding of the purpose, and even the value, of ambivalence.

The more obvious pitfall is in the way some moralists insist that men can discriminate clearly between good and evil as long as they are honest and sincerely motivated. This ignores the experiential fact that men often are, in spite of the best motives, unable to do so. Many of the practices which these people believe to be morally beneficial — confession for the Catholic, to cite one specific example — often lead nowhere. Psychology has shown that men often tend to impose moral sanctions on themselves or others because they are afraid to admit confusion. The "sense of responsibility" which preoccupies some men can be an escape from what is, at best, uncertainty and ambivalence of motive. Some moralists would have us believe that ambivalence is always a sign of weakness. They cannot accept the possibility that ambivalence might have a positive function in experience.

From a psychotheological vantage, there is a great deal of value in those instances where man cannot discriminate between good and evil, or between what is healthy or neurotic. Christ clearly recognized this, and on a number of occasions emphasized the importance of accepting it as part of experience. A good illustration is in the parable of the good and bad seed:

> "The kingdom of heaven may be compared to a man who sowed good seed in his field. While everybody was asleep his enemy came, sowed darnel all among the wheat, and made off. When the new wheat sprouted and ripened, the darnel appeared as well. The owner's servants went to him and said, 'Sir, was it not good seed that you sowed in your field? If so, where does the darnel come from?' 'Some enemy has done this,' he answered. And the servants said, 'Do you want us to go and weed it out?' But he said, 'No, because when you weed out the darnel you might pull up the wheat with it. Let them both grow till the harvest; and at harvest time I shall say to the reapers: First collect the darnel and tie it in bundles to be burnt; then gather the wheat into my barn' " (Matthew 13, 24-30).

A strictly religious interpretation delimits this passage and may overlook the value of the enigma it points to. For example, it has been used to justify predestination, the belief that a certain segment of the human race is irremediably doomed to destruction. Or, on a more sophisticated level, it may interpret the field as the heart of man where both evil and goodness grow, and where, presumably, the good will overcome the evil. In either case, the psychological subtlety of the passage is overlooked.

The wisdom expressed in this parable consists in its implicit recognition that the neurotic and the unhealthy have at least a temporary right to life, and thus they must somehow spring from the same source as healthy life. It presents this as an irrevocable fact of experience. From a psychospiritual point of view, we might say that before man can make free moral choices or become morally sensitive, he has to be psychologically aware of the risk that should accompany every value judgment.

Experience again seems to corroborate Christ's words on another level. The healthy and the sick are often disguised to look alike; they may be interchangeable or intimately related. What was yesterday's useless weed becomes, by grace of evolution, tomorrow's fruitful plant. The misfits of society may turn out to be its prophets; today's enemy, tomorrow's ally. This is not simply another indication of how experience plays tricks on us. It is life's way of refusing our constant attempts to straitjacket experience when we should be allowing it to unfold.

But do not our moral instincts tell us that there are moments when we must distinguish between good and evil? Even the most permissive, non-directive therapy realizes that at some moment indecision must give way to action. In our age especially, moral indifferentism seems intolerable. The issues are too important, we say. We cannot be forever reassured by therapist, priest, or politician that all will turn out well as long as we are patient. Our own moral blindspots and the evil manifested in others must be recognized and eradicated for the moral danger they pose.

But the psychotheological point is that when such moral judgments are made about ourselves or others they can never be simply *condemnatory;* they must always be *appreciative* in the fullest sense of the word. Even moral judgment can be used as an expedient. Destructiveness for whatever motive can never have any real function in the life of a mature man, who is guided only by the hope of possible enlightenment. The moralist, perhaps more than anyone, must learn that the growth of human personality can never be achieved solely by judging it. Being moral means not only learning how to judge but also allowing the disparate elements in human experience to reveal how men can become more mature.

The only other choice is arrogance, rigidifying one's life in the name of morality. This is the stance of the pharisee, the witch-hunter, the inquisitor. The supermoralist shuts his heart to the sense of ambivalence because he puts moralism before moral sensitivity, his own or others. His judgments, whether rendered in the name of religion or politics, are inevitably condemnatory.

This kind of moralism amputates itself from the rest of mankind because it regards itself above the process of moral evolution. What binds men together psychologically, however, is the admission that individual consciences can be limited by ignorance and arrogance. One begins to understand more clearly why Christ was so harsh with the dogmatism of his own co-religionists.

When Christ spoke of letting the darnel grow along with the wheat, he was warning us of our tendency to the arrogance which dictates that we must destroy what we cannot understand or don't like. To the true Christian the moral demands that Christ makes can never be destructive. True Christians recognize that men's instincts are involved in a common quest for convergence. They look to the day when men will have achieved a cosmic moral sense based on their need for each other and their love for one another in confusion or clarity. Thus psychotheology can view moral ambivalence as a step in mankind's search for a universal moral sense.

If man finds such a goal to be distant, it is because he attaches great importance to the conditioning and pre-conditioning of his particular environment. Moral insight is only spasmodically achieved and comes only through trial, error and bitter experience. Most of us are slaves of our own religious and nationalistic propaganda. As psychotheology sees it, the future of morality will always depend upon the extent to which religious practice helps men develop an organic kinship with all of life.

Moral Insight

All great ethical systems have sought moral convergence. Beatific vision, cosmic consciousness, the *Kenchu-to* of Zen Buddhism — each reflects man's desire for a single moral vision for the human race.

The steps leading to this state have been variously conceived. For the man of the East, the practice of Yoga or Zen aims at "losing" consciousness in order to attain a pure consciousness or "formless self." For the Jew and the Christian, it consists in perfecting the Covenant between God and man, sacralizing time and human relationships. East and West meet at the point where moral choice means accepting a psychological paradox which requires that a man must lose in order to find, become weak in order to be strong, be poor in order to become rich. Both demand the moral courage to seek light from darkness, clarity out of confusion, to leap from one state to a higher one.

This bears on what we have been saying. We can understand paradox only when we accept ambivalence. Christ's paradoxes reflect not moral confusion but fruitful psychological contradictions which frequently lead to newer and deeper insights. "Love your enemy," Christ commands; this demands acceptance of the paradox that it is at least possible that those whom we think are our enemies may finally be no threat to us at all.

Christ's injunction demands that we have the moral courage to face the psychological pain of discarding an earlier sense of what was true. A new insight makes an old prejudice superfluous. The purpose of psychoanalysis, according to Freud, was to make the unconscious conscious so that consciousness might be transformed into something more nearly representing the fully functioning man. In fact, in an evolutionary scheme, reversion to old life patterns is not merely retrogressive but almost always evil. When the Nazis reverted to barbarism, we did not blame them just for being non-progressive. The God of the Old Testament meted out punishments for relapses into forms of idolatry. Man's yearning for cosmic morality teeters on the brink of catastrophe whenever he is tempted, like Lot's wife, to look back.

Classic psychology offers two major explanations of how consciousness of reality deepens, and both have a bearing on the growth of moral consciousness. The first says that the acquisition of knowledge is achieved by trial and error — learning by mistakes. Other psychologists maintain that the growth of consciousness consists in sudden leaps of insight, or "gestalts," whereby truth is achieved not so much by a logical analysis of a given situation, but by sudden flashes of revelation. Given a blurred set of shapes we tend to project form. Out of inkblots we make butterflies or witches dancing in a ring. Man, according to the latter view, has a strong inclination to see experience in organized wholes.

Psychologists have hesitated to apply these theories to ethical behavior because they are doubtful that men's moral drives can be measured the way psychological reactions can. But in our context, psychic activity and moral behavior are seen from a single viewpoint — what experience reveals about the human heart. For psychotheology, psychological theories of perception and the deepening of human sensitivity, then, are vital to understanding the nature of moral inquiry. There is no reason why such theories, if they have any validity, should not be brought to bear upon the question of moral behavior.

Taking the first theory into consideration, for example, most men presume that there must be constant trial-and-error in order to develop satisfactory ethical behavior. Thus they learn to tolerate neurotic and immoral forms of behavior, viewing them as means — however distasteful — to achieve a greater end.

But it is also possible to be moral in a way that does not depend upon mistakes, a way that transcends even the rational demands of an ethical system. Men do seek moments when they reach to fulfill their impulses from sheer moral compulsion — when, for example, the fulfillment of the supreme law of moral unity, to love all men, is affirmed as being independent of any rational process. A racist can never be convinced logically that all men are worthy of his love. Experience has shown that man's moral sense grows by education, but also that men are attracted to moral ideals because of what Pascal called the "reasons of the heart." Psychotheologically, this is an experience of *moral gestalt*. This is not to say that there is something magical about the growth in moral sensitivity, but only that a man can become more morally alive in ways that he himself does not fully understand.

Christ testified to the validity of this experience when he declared that the man who believes without proof is somehow more blessed than the man who has proof. New kinds of "seeing" are available only to the man who accepts the challenge to rise from the narrowly obvious to new levels of moral awareness. Christ had such a moral power; if we do not, it is because the sense of confusion we experience in our moral quest did not threaten him the way it threatens us.

The possibility of moral insight reassures man that he can achieve a sense of moral purpose. It also gives him reason to hope for a new age of a moral vision universally shared. Christianity stresses this millennial concept only because Christ said it was possible. If psychology has not dealt too kindly with the idea, it is because it has not been able to measure the psychological validity of such a concept in the here-and-now to its own satisfaction. The prospect of a day when a universal moral sense will have evolved is, to the empirical mind, dim indeed.

For this reason psychotheology insists that the great apocalyptic texts of the New Testament must be reassessed in a psychological context and taken beyond the level of a kind of divine prophecy which has no pertinence in human affairs. There must be, in short, a phenomenological appreciation of Christ's millennial teachings. In this way they may be raised to a level of psychospiritual sophistication which the secularist mind cannot find in them now. In this context God becomes the Ultimate Gestalt, the power without which the moral and psychological drives of mankind, whether taken individually or collectively, cannot be understood.

Men's moral and psychological drives cannot converge without reference to a larger scheme, without faith in the possibility of an Ultimate Gestalt. This is because experience testifies to our strong tendency to preserve security at all costs. We need the pull of a transcendent goal to get us past our resistances to change. If we lack hope in a single moral destiny, differences can lead us to chaos as easily as to convergence. In short, our behavior takes on significance only to the extent that we see it intimately linked with the desire of other men to achieve a single moral destiny for the human race.

To have confidence in such a goal means that experience has revealed that there are patterns of unity in human behavior, as there are in nature, which link men to each other, patterns which are revealed only through time and experience. Men can make moral leaps in a world where progress, and not merely process, is possible.

The fact that we are faced constantly with conflict indicates the existence of a still fragmented sense of morality. But men nevertheless continue to experience the desire for real union with each other. A man who suddenly understands that his needs are the same as those of all other men has in a real sense experienced the miraculous. He has reached a new moral dimension — one which discovers the command to "love your neighbor as yourself" as the greatest insight available, a psychospiritual imperative which no man can pretend to understand through the power of logic alone.

That some men sense the need for moral unity more than others is a mystery. The journey toward moral unity is rarely smooth; it is not a continuum but a jagged line. Still, the morality of actions is recognizable at least in those moments and in those situations which demand a vital, conscious response to the needs of others. If tolerance is mankind's greatest hope, then timidity is its worst enemy. Hesitation, not confusion, perpetuates the fragmented sense of morality that racks the world. Every man is guilty of neglect when he openly denies a sense of responsibility toward his fellow man; but the more insidious sin is on the part of those who claim to have the vision but who refuse to take the risks.

The Christian says that he looks to Christ as his personal ideal. Fundamentally, this means that he recognizes the Christ of the New Testament as a person who believed that all men can become better than they think they are. This is evident in his moral commands which are fully consonant with man's psychological needs and with the laws of growth and experience. But ultimately the most profound relevance of Christ for modern man is what it has always been: that he confirmed by his own life the dynamic principle that all men are members of one another. The convergence that each man experiences in his individual life, when he discovers that moral aspiration and psychic impulse are one, reflects Christ's deeper promise of cosmic convergence. To believe that we can love one another the way Christ loved us means achieving the greatest insight mankind can experience in its journey toward universal morality and harmony.

3

THE INCARNATION AND HUMAN CONSCIOUSNESS

The task of psychotheology is to relate the psychological insights of the 20th century with the basic tenets of Christian mystery. The task is not easy. In the last chapter we saw that Christ's command to love one another can be understood best in the light of what psychology and religion tell us about the human hope for unity, and that only love can produce the unity. Yet psychotheology finds an even deeper basis for Christ's moral injunction to love one another. The basis can be found in the very nature of his relationship to God, with its profound psychological, as well as religious, implications.

Incarnation

Christian theology has traditionally maintained that Christ's presence can be experienced in a number of ways — in the eucharist, for example, and for Catholics in the teaching authority of the Church. (Of course this latter example has been disputed since the Reformation. Much more rethinking needs to be done if we are ever to appreciate how the power of Christ can work through an institution.) Finally there is the great and unmistakable sign of Christ's presence in the world (unmistakable because of the psychological power of his words): "Where two or three meet in my name, I shall be there with them" (Matthew 18, 20).

Psychotheology considers the simple messages of the Gospel in conjunction with what we have come to learn about the operations of the human mind and heart. In the discussion of human brotherhood and the relationship of men to one another, Christian belief in the Incarnation lends itself most fruitfully to psychotheological analysis, for it is precisely here that we can find the message of Christian love most clearly revealed with stunning psychological force. It is found on the most essential level — converging in the person of Christ, the level of human longing and divine fulfillment.

This issue must be explicated not by balancing the supernatural against the natural, but on a level where what is a revealed mystery finds its ultimate meaning reflected in human experience. This argument does not denigrate the transcendent meaning of God. It is an attempt to show that when we speak of man as the "image" of God, we must, in some way, attempt to find psychological verification for what we accept on faith.

Some years ago, the French historian of philosophy Etienne Gilson attacked St. Anselm precisely on this score. Gilson saw clearly that St. Anselm was looking for psychological verification for Christian mystery, and he accused him of being a reckless rationalist. But as we pointed out earlier, the phenomenological tradition in modern Christian thinking has once again assumed the eminence it had lost with the ascendance of Thomistic Scholasticism. Anselm, by trying to give empirical verification to faith as a force whereby man tries to understand the impulses of his own heart in the light of revelation, can no longer be dismissed as an adventurer who tried to water down the "supernatural" aspects of revelation. Rather, he was searching for a place where psychological longing and Christian mystery converge; he was trying to understand mystery in terms of human experience. Of no great Christian mystery can this process be more fruitful than the Incarnation.

In a sense, God was always incarnate in that he always manifested himself in one way or other through his creation. The myriad testimony of religions before Christianity attests to this in varying ways. Incarnation is a special act with the specific purpose of bringing man's inner consciousness in touch with God. In psychotheological terms this is accomplished by giving man the opportunity to confront God himself. It was the mission of Christ to help us understand through our own consciousness what we had in some sense always intuited — that a Power moves among men. Incarnation means that man now becomes more conscious of the world as the environment for working out his destiny.

God expresses himself in human form through the developing process of human consciousness, through knowing and thinking. A child springs from a common heritage, a collective, unconscious matrix over which he has little control and of which he is scarcely aware. Yet as the child's life unfolds within the particular circumstances of his family, he is all the while learning to appreciate his mysterious patrimony. So too the presence of Christ points to the mysterious presence of God who dwells in the depths of creation. Through Christ, God reveals his presence in existence in the only meaningful way — *on the level of man's consciousness.* God produced an image of himself by means of a human conscious nature, or — to go beyond the historical Christ — he chose humanity on the level he created it in order to raise it to his level. He wanted to show in the clearest terms that he does indeed dwell among men, not as an occasional visitor from Olympus, or only in the beauty of the world, but by being born in time, in a particular place, in the flesh.

This is of paramount importance. All human experiences, those understood now and those yet to be comprehended by evolving consciousness, help to illuminate the purpose of life. The Incarnation, far from being an exception or (as it has been for many) a stumbling block, gives assurance that the impulses of the human heart are valid. To put it in psychotheological terms, this is a point where religious mystery and human experience converge.

The Incarnation must be seen, first of all, to transcend the historical event of some 2,000 years ago. The Christ whom God revealed had always been working in creation and in the human heart. But for man, Christ's incarnation became Incarnation, revealing the possibility of new levels of divine activity in his conscious relations with life around him. What we say here can be laid down as a principle for the entire psychotheological approach: If *revelare* means "to take away the veil" from God's face, it means taking it away from man's heart as well.

Human incarnational activity invariably takes appropriate forms. A man's affective sense seeks keener fulfillment by immersion in a world of people and objects which had previously been partly obscured. Until then he had been "seeing a dim reflection in a mirror" (1 Corinthians 13, 12), but with the vision of Christ everything becomes alive with the majesty intended for it. His need to perfect his image and that of the world allows him to understand the need for and possibility of the Incarnation as psychologically meaningful.

It is precisely when man fails to see that life is morally and psychologically important that he loses hope and inspiration. Thus the "sense of the incarnate," rather than being a sign of mankind's frustrated desire for apotheosis, is a symbol of the fulfillment everyone seeks — the need to become more than what we think we are. All disciplines which have striven to define this longing affirm the premise that all human energy is an attempt to bring meaning to our feelings of dissociation.

Even the study of parapsychology can, if it gets beyond the statistical stage, enhance man's understanding of how the divine moves among us. We are able to perceive God's presence as foreshadowed in countless ways. We can think, for example, of those experiences we do not understand — those mysterious occurrences we call "chance" or "coincidence" — events whose origins are so mysterious that we cannot classify them rationally. Both religion and psychology have difficulty handling them, but the psychotheological approach, committed as it is to experience, at least allows for the possibility that they are of some intrinsic worth. Human speculation on any level can lead to a discovery of God's limitless presence in human enterprise. This does not detract from what the Christian community has traditionally understood about Incarnation in its historical sense as the presence of Christ in the world, begun solely and uniquely with his appearance on earth; for it is precisely here that the historical event gives substance to the claim that it is the dynamic focal point for any future sense of incarnation.

The convergence of human and divine was made manifest in time but — and this is the psychotheological point — *the Incarnation, whatever it means in eternity, can make no sense apart from human consciousness.* It is the crucial moment in God's plan to sanctify creation and "to open the gates of heaven." It bridges the gulf human consciousness could never span, catalyzing the most important step in man's evolutionary journey: the awakening of man's consciousness to the realization that his yearnings for the Transcendent are not in vain. Looked at from this point of view, theological arguments such as "If man had not sinned, God would not have come" become superfluous. The Incarnation becomes rather a necessary step in evolution for the Christian, since through the person of Christ become man the human race could proceed to a newer and deeper consciousness of itself. We saw earlier how the story of Eden can be viewed as a depiction of man's coming to consciousness. The argument about whether man "had to sin or not" did not concern us then, and need not now. Psychotheology asserts that the Incarnation need not be merely an abstract theological battlefield on which God's power is to be jealously guarded at all costs, but a focal point of paramount importance in the evolution of human consciousness.

The corollary that the sense of Incarnation expands only as long as man's consciousness expands is an even more startling insight. The Incarnation of Christ asserts that human life can be lived to its fullest degree only in the consciously felt presence of God. Christ saw that man's participation in and acceptance of this belief is the only ground on which human potentials can develop, for it demands that through his evolving self-love and recognition man become more intimately related with and immersed in the world he is meant to mold. Man does live in a divine milieu, and the more he learns of his inner conscious life, the better he is able to decipher the incarnational energy on every level of human consciousness; perhaps someday he may even be able to do so on the level of his own unconscious and superconscious. "I am with you always" (Matthew 28, 20), Christ said before his leave-taking. And we might add, "on all levels of human experience," past, present and to come.

The opening up of the human personality with the advent of Freud has come full circle, from seeing Christian mystery as illusory to viewing its mythic dimension as pervading the deepest level of man's being.

Psychic Resistances to Incarnation

Since it is man's present consciousness with which we are concerned, it would be foolish to think that the human sense of incarnation justifies accepting the Christian mystery. For many persons, the mystery of the Incarnation will always be a hopeless contradiction. Every century of religious and philosophical development, our own included, reveals a resistance within the heart of man to the notion that God can communicate with his creatures in a way which would limit him. Most philosophic or religious systems define God as utterly transcendent, nameless, beyond human capture. For this reason the Incarnation has been comprehended only with difficulty by people such as the Orientals. At times their atavistic teachings seem to lean toward the Christian tradition, but even the avatars of Vishnu are caught up in an eternal cycle and remain timeless. Certainly this is one Christian truth that is highly susceptible to human doubt. (And we are all potential atheists in that we will accept only what we consider to be a purist notion of God.) Even the Western mind with its secular humanist heritage favors the comfortably rational and the obvious in human consciousness, rejecting anything that approaches the intuitive. St. Thomas Aquinas, for example, for all the distinguishing and counter-distinguishing in his defense against the logical objections to the Incarnation, is still too much of a rationalist to see how the mystery was more than merely a revelation to be defended and developed on its own grounds. For Thomas and other rationalists, poetic insight, or the power of the human mind to discover truth on an intuitive level, was always the least important mental activity. For many of us, the significance of symbolism, poetry and even magic and superstition have been constricted by the narrowness of a basically empirical cosmology. That being said, it would seem that the essential, immediate difficulty with the incarnational mystery is not so much in its abstract paradoxes or in man's refusal to consent to it intellectually, but in man's lack of an *experiential* basis upon which to consider it. That is a most serious objection, and it is one that psychotheology has to confront.

The objection tends to lose its force, however, when one sees that the so-called "leap" to faith in revealed mystery (made so much of by traditional theologians) can and does occur in the case of the Incarnation when one recognizes the sacredness of another person. The fact that there is another encourages one to entertain the possibility of God's having an animate form. Belief in the Incarnation for the modern man can be founded only on such experience. Psychological resistance to the personification of God occurs only to the extent that we think that humanity is sourceless. The sense of the Holy becomes palpable only when man sees flesh as in some way sacred. Only then can belief in the Incarnation become a psychological as well as a religious force. As always, psychotheology falls back on the principle that *man experiences and thus believes*. It is never the other way around.

The Incarnation and Relational Morality

In attempting to see another person as worthy of our love and respect, we are opened up to an even more challenging mystery — that of God as Community. Incarnation cannot be discussed apart from this question. For the Trinity, seemingly the most incomprehensible of religious paradoxes, becomes more understandable when we see the relationship the Incarnation bears to it. One mystery illuminates the other. The person of Christ finds his fullest significance in the notion of God as Community.

Theologians have explored the concept of the trinitarian nature of God from their own vantage points. But today, phenomenologically, we are in a better position to understand how the notion of God as Community does touch upon humanity's growth and development.

Theological discussions (both those for and against a trinitarian definition) have tended to substitute abstract reasoning for experience, and in this sense they necessarily fall short of advancing our understanding of how God manifests himself in the life of men. For it is only by defining God as community that humans can bring themselves to accept the importance of community. The definition of God as Trinity becomes more than just another incomprehensible idea that some may consider *démodé*. It gives a cohesiveness and a deeper meaning to everything we have said about the relationship of Christ to God, of Christ to man, and of men to each other. It gives a profounder meaning to our concept of society itself.

According to the famous psychologist William McDougall, an organized group is always a "work group" and never one built simply on "basic assumptions." The notion of community demands a notion of interactive cooperation. Even the notion of God must go beyond our "basic assumptions" about him. If it did not, we would never get beyond the typical theological discussion of the Trinity as a kind of mathematical puzzle. The Trinity is more than the Christian definition of God; rather, it is a symbolic way of describing the very nature of divine energy. This means that God can never be described as static. Like man, the only way to express anything about him is in terms of the action of community. Western thinking, from the Greeks to the medieval Scholastics, has always been troubled by this dilemma. Plato, in the tradition of Heraclitus, saw God in terms of energy and self-diffusing light, while Aristotle made him into a mover who is unmoved. In the 13th century Aquinas and Bonaventure came to loggerheads over the question in almost the same way. But today we have come to see that the Aristotelian-Thomistic tradition is no answer to what modern man, at least since Spinoza, wants to believe about God and his relation to the world. Modern man has attempted to see creation as more than a projection of a divine narcissism and God as more than a power who seeks merely to be glorified. We speak now of God as a "Thou" who communicates and who calls upon his creation to emulate himself in his desire for cooperative, relational activity. As far as 20th-century man is concerned, simple adoration of God as an object is less important than encountering him through some person, persons or group. It was the dynamic vision of the early Protestant reformers, who rejected the idea that activity is aimed solely and quintessentially at the *visio dei,* that led to the eventual breakup of the accepted medieval notion that the worship of God was contemplation alone. The radical reorientation of the definition of God as a force who calls upon man to act set modern man on his course of rebuilding the earth. We are only too aware of what this led to socially, economically, and — in America especially — politically. Our entire democratic structure was built upon this principle, with results that only the most critical enemies of democracy have cared to criticize. Certain Christians — most notably Catholics — even while living in such a society, have nevertheless been obsessed with the fear of neglecting God as an object of adoration if they should attempt to see him in terms of process and energy. They, perhaps more than any others, epitomize Rilke's complaint about the man who "almost forgot God over the hard work of drawing near him."

Within a psychotheological context then, the mystery of the Trinity must somehow be linked with the sense of community. What other meaning, even in our limited understanding, could such a mystery have? Traditional theology speaks about the "inner relations of the Trinity," but it is more interesting for us to consider that if God is community, he is so because of our association with him. Just as the organic parts of the body work together in the life process, so too in all of his psychological and social complexity man is *most fully* man when he is sharing and cooperating. When the members of the community fail to act in concert, it is just as destructive of life as if the cells, tissues and organs of the body were to act at cross-purposes. When they do cooperate, the community becomes a large whole, a new unity. The process continues when several communities in society unite. The Gestalt is always greater than the parts; the Gestalt becomes something in itself.

The objection to this point of view is that we run the risk of denying the rights and personalities of individual natures. But cer-

tainly no one can fail to see that it is only the whole that makes
each part ultimately understandable. If we want a complete vision
of what man is, we must see him in all of his relations.

Only through association and alliance does any individual nature
become particularized and understood. As Rousseau saw, man
takes on the characteristics of man only as he contributes to the
community that ensures his survival. Human experience has borne
out the requirement for communing with and through social groups.
Friendship, family, national and world allegiance, identification
with the cosmos, and — more particularly today — the presence
of scattered charismatic groups are all manifestations of the necessity of community for fostering personality fulfillment. The individual becomes greater than himself by aligning with an aggregate,
and if love and human desire have any meaning in a century widely
proclaimed as "godless," they must point to the fact that even we
are trying to become greater than ourselves.

Cooperation with others does not detract from selfhood. "Anyone who loses his life for my sake shall find it," Christ said, and
here he was paying tribute to a dynamic principle of human personality development on both a moral and psychological level. He
was not merely exhorting us to the value of ascetical practice. He
saw that it is only by broadening one's experience that the renewal
and expansion of the individual self becomes possible.

We can understand how the human appreciation of a divine
community can be verified in the idea of group. We have been told
that the natural human unit is the family. We understand it better
when we consider that even the family is based on more than a
one-to-one relationship. The father-mother-child unit is more complete than merely the father-mother or the individual parent-child
relationship. Our sense of the divine community becomes verifi-
able through our appreciation of family, of brotherhood.

Some theologians may object to these comments on the Trinity.
They have always been jealous to guard the unique nature of God
while asserting the individual *operations* of the three persons.
Psychotheology, however, refuses to enter into such abstractions.
The world of the Son may be different from the world of the Father
or the breadth of the Holy Spirit. They represent "portions" of God,

aspects of God's overall being, much as the many worlds of each person contribute to the whole man. God too, in short, is co-action. Each person of God is in himself entire, yet there is an accordance and harmony, a radical relationship of love and activity which makes them a single community. Man, God's highest creation, mirrors this community, for man was made in God's image.

Here the psychological value of the Incarnation becomes abundantly clear. The Incarnation showed creation that its existence is basically relational or societal, that man can understand very little about himself or the world except in relation to God, to other men, and to the world about him. Rationalistic Western philosophy, starting with Aristotle, has always viewed the concept of "relation" as being accidental or unimportant, too mixed up with contingencies. But the mystery of the Incarnation tells us that God is linked to humanity precisely because of a radical relational activity, which is the essence of his inner life and the means by which he relates to us. Relational activity is necessary for man to understand himself because it is the very milieu in which he is created and continues to operate. Man's continuing development, indeed his survival, depends upon the extent to which he learns to love the community, in all its distinctive variety, as the ground of his personality.

In *The City of God,* St. Augustine stresses the fact that a harmonious relationship with one's fellows comes only after one has achieved a relationship with God. The psychotheological theme is in essence the same: An individual is able to recognize the moral necessity of his relationships only in terms of his experience with others. It is in early life, particularly in a child's relations with significant adults, that his course is set. If his associations with them are unsatisfactory, what follows will always manifest itself in the still unresolved conflicts of childhood. Until one has some key to one's sources, a person is at a loss to operate in the community at large. An individual who feels a neurotic sense of unworthiness is not prepared to accept the stress of more extended relationships. He may be overly defensive or withdrawn. Augustine's insight was not merely pious exhortation. He was emphasizing that sense of feeling in the Christian community which can and must be grounded in a mystery, which would give man the power and strength to cope with all that he has to face in life. Only an individual who sees that his moral and psychic life is grounded in the community will understand in his very marrow that this individuality is merely an opportunity or invitation to participate more fully and securely within the social group. The religiously mature person sees the community as the only medium for his individuation. Uniqueness is meaningless outside a group. As he is immersed in a community, he comes to the realization that he is not only a member of a larger group, but a member within that group. He finds his own identity mirrored in his experience with others. As he becomes more deeply involved, the community becomes an extension of home and his individuality is uncovered even more clearly. Harmony by its very nature requires many parts. It is dependent not on similarity but differences, and it consists in the degree of communication and exchange between the components. It is the same with Christ, whose uniqueness among men pre-necessitated his becoming man. His unique role in the divine community is a direct function of his participation in its unity.

Through his Incarnation God has revealed himself as a member of our species. In a psychotheological context, even biology becomes sacred when we consider that by entering the human community God demonstrated man's connaturality with the divine community. It is irrelevant at this point to invoke the traditional distinction between supernatural and natural, as if the two communities were disparate. The truth is that one is the image of the other, and between the truth and the imaging of it there can be no danger of confusion between kind.

Ultimately, Incarnation makes no sense except in light of the deeper truth that all morality rests upon the notion of community. There are no Christian moral principles operative outside a sense of community. In the long run all the great moral arenas are social. The morally alive person attempts to correlate his inmost spiritual intuitions with the great mysteries and tries to show how they can be verified through experience.

Only within the social structure (the family in its widest sense) can men begin to achieve their full potential. This is an important experiential truth because it corresponds with everything entailed by faith. Christians are not obliged to respect their community and their brothers as a matter of choice but as a metaphysical necessity for survival. What this means in Christian terms is that they are called upon to see that Incarnation, the focal point of their religion, is forever a reminder that incarnation is available to them at all times. How else can man see even his own physical existence except as a community, with every part of his own body dependent upon the whole for its life? The analogy does not say that man's sense of community is automatic or can be achieved mechanically by social or economic forces. Every attempt at union demands freedom, love, patience and perseverance. Through the rhythmic exchange of the giver and receiver God touches and opens up humanity and the world. As we have received, so do we give. The psychodynamic principle enunciated by Christ — "there is more happiness in giving than receiving" — bears full application here.

God has given himself to humanity, and in revealing his intimate relation to it he has radically *touched* it. By touching humanity, by drawing a Christ out from it, God's purpose was to help man discover himself. Through the "touch" of the Incarnation, God communicated with man, excited the affections of the human heart, and helped men to see himself as a social being.

Theology has always been threatened by the suggestion that God's "touching" of creation, bringing forth what was latent in it, would tempt man to detract from God's self-sufficiency, immutability and absolute transcendence. However, God is never limited by his creation, any more than our personalities are destroyed by the words we utter, by our participation in a community, by the children we bear. Rather, through these events our personalities are glorified, further revealed. The human struggle is not so much to change and adjust as it is to fulfill ultimate capacities. The word "fulfillment" can be used of both God and man in this sense without fear of either anthropomorphism *or* apotheosis. If man's fulfillment is unfolded in time, God's has been for all eternity. And if logical distinctions collapse at this point, it is only because abstract thinking has failed to understand the deeper applications of the concept of analogy.

The word "touch" must be taken in the most intimate sense of its meaning. The element of touch has always been central in the Christian tradition, and modern psychology is beginning to show why. On many occasions Christ transmitted his divine power of healing through touch. Through the centuries, touch has figured predominantly in the sacramental activities of Christianity — the laying on of hands in baptism, confirmation, and in the conferring of holy orders, among others. Indeed, the entire basis of the apostolic tradition, some Christians believe, consists in the touch of the bishop's hands on the candidate for ordination. There is a vitality in a touch which eludes description. To touch is in a real sense *to give birth,* for touch heralds new beginnings and is the symbol of restoration to a new life.

Similarly, primitive psychological systems of healing always emphasized contact. The palpitations and fevers that besiege us are necessary preparations for the healing touch whereby we are drawn out of ourselves, as God draws Christ from our midst.

Human experience shows that we are indeed capable of being radically affected by touches from "without." Man becomes psychotic if he fails to deal with the world of experience on a workable conscious level. Human beings may be attuned to grasp only a limited range to which their senses are geared, yet something outside can touch the world within and help it to expand. In modern thought even the theory of the so-called "limitation" of our senses is being seriously questioned.

Nevertheless there is much resistance to understanding how healing and fruitful touch really is. This undoubtedly stems from all the taboos attached to it in the long tradition of orthodox asceticism. In the 20th century, however, many breakthroughs have been made. Psychologist Henry Guze has attempted to show, for example, that one of the most effective therapies consists of the psychotherapist's ability to locate physically the center of a patient's anxiety. As he recognizes clues, the clinician himself becomes more sensitive. People reveal themselves at their most profound levels through hunger, tightness, headaches, even blindness. The warmth of another's concern and contact is frequently enough to liberate the tenseness which has kept the person chained.

In dealing with man, God works within the limitations of man's consciousness, but as that consciousness expands, so too does man's understanding of his relationship to his fellow man. At one stage of our evolutionary development, we were touched by God, and as we proceed to further stages, Incarnation will take on a newer and deeper illumination. There was a beginning, and presumably there will be some kind of end to man, but Christ as the perfect expression of man will continue forever.

Creation existed before man entered into it, but once he did he was caught up in the evolutionary unfolding of the universe. While man has inborn limitations, he is perpetually freeing himself from those that enslave him. When he reaches what Teilhard calls the "Omega Point," he will have progressed to a point where even his own sense of limitation becomes meaningless. Man transcends his limitations only as he recognizes his dynamic relationship to the living God through the saving power of the community. When that struggle ceases and the world freely expresses the unity and peace of God, enslavement will no longer be necessary. The encounter will have reached its complete fulfillment and unfolding.

Incarnation includes the manifest reality that God and man have encountered each other in Christ in a perfect way. That relationship is the archetype of all divine-human relations. But even Christ's relationship to the Father, insofar as his human consciousness is concerned, was not static. He, too, had to develop a sense of community in a human way. He is our model precisely because he showed us how we should deepen the awareness in ourselves. Our task is to share this experience in our own lives. We must be able to see on any level of human experience how this is at least possible, if not always immediately apparent. Here again, psychology has illuminated Christian mystery.

Andras Angyal, in outlining his psychology of personality, spoke of the concept of "super-individuality." He traced the growth of human consciousness through the process of increasing human units. The newly born is helpless and dependent; but as it grows, it manages to reach out and up, thus creating some sense, however inchoate, of union. Later the force of family comes into play, then the larger community, and finally friendship with the cosmos itself.

Likewise, Christ's participation in the divine community, the archetypal symbol of our own, is based on the fact that super-individuality is an available experience for all of us. Indeed the entire foundation for the psychotheological view is the fact that super-individuality is the only way man has of communing. No concept of man's moral or psychological nature can exclude the essential fact of community. Christ knew this, and if Incarnation has any meaning it must bring with it the palpable, visible brotherhood fashioned after the divine community which Christ knew. "May they all be one. Father, may they be one in us, as you are in me and I am in you" (John 17, 21).

Christ's anguish in the garden and his apparent indecision and anxiety before the ultimate test of his crucifixion point to the inevitability of a sense of ambivalence between the divine and the human. There must be tension and struggle in man's search for the divine. In Christ's case there was no open conflict or evasion as with us, yet like any man Christ was not always free of ambivalence. Or, to put it more precisely, he was not always in touch with his unconscious. The God element in him may not have been apparent to him at all times. He did not always "see" in the fullest sense during his human sojourn before the resurrection. He had to undergo the experience of Gethsemane in order to see clearly what the will of God was for him.

When St. Paul said that Christ was like us in all things save sin, he certainly did not mean to exclude him from the human situation. Rather, he intended to heighten our understanding of Christ's humanity. We become aware that it may have been impossible for him always to confront or understand the full implications of his relationship to God. Since he was human, Christ must have shared in many shortsighted aspects of human nature. He had to struggle like any mortal to achieve his goals. There were times when he allowed his sense of union with God to possess him completely, as when he was transfigured before his disciples. But an insight such as this pointed only to one thing: the coming ultimate and total apotheosis of his humanity at the moment of resurrection.

Christ's vision of God was like ours, but infinitely more futuristic and perfect. In his expansiveness and freedom from any trace of willful moral corruption, he was supremely competent in the panorama of human activities which went to make up his thirty-odd years on earth. His vision, his consciousness, destined from the beginning for perfect fulfillment, allowed him to penetrate the score of human possibilities, since he alone was capable of trusting and allowing the full potential of his consciousness free rein.

Some theologians inform us that the human Christ always knew he was a member of the divine community. This knowledge was "infused," they say, from the moment of his conception. This does not tell us much from a psychotheological point of view, for we are interested in Christ's growing consciousness of his own identity with and through the Trinity. His knowledge of union with the divine was no different from his acquaintance with his Father on a superhuman level. And yet, like us, his knowledge of God emerged as his consciousness of being human grew. What does strike us from a psychotheological point of view is the way in which Christ handled the ambivalence — not as a sign of opposition or even enmity between God and man but as an opportunity for entering more deeply into the life of God, to be possessed rather than to possess. From this we see that our communion with God must in some way be reflected in Christ's relation to God in his humanity. This is for us the only purpose of the Incarnation. It shows us in what way all men, as well as Christ himself, are related to God. It emphasizes, perhaps more than any other aspect of his life and teaching, what he meant when he told us that he was "the Way."

For a Christian, the archetypal relationship of Christ to God reminds us that we are like Christ, open to the wealth of God's inner life and truth. Christ's mission was to awaken man's consciousness to this fact. It was he who freed mankind from the "elemental principles of this world" (Galatians 4, 3), from the limitations of our experience by which we too easily bound our horizons.

In some unique way Christ is what each of us is. He was man; so are we. He was "the most beautiful of the sons of men," and we share in the possibility of this perfection. Incarnation shows us that through Christ we are all sons because we are all brothers. The years that Christ lived on earth were the means of showing this to the human race. It was his mission to make the human race aware of its bloodline with God, to show us to what hidden treasures we are heirs. To those of us who participate freely in the legacy he left behind, this is the only reality, and it is one that we discover only through Christ's life and teaching. Christ is the *only* man, the first man ever really created. He is the firstborn of our Father. In his love we see the ideal embodiment of utter trust, utter love, the glorification of God's creation to the fullest. He is the fulfillment of what every man hopes to be.

Christ was also firstborn in the sense that he had a right to speak to his Father. But that right is now ours. What is more important is that he earned it precisely because he met the ultimate test — which is that a man will give all for those he loves and for the community in which he lives. Christ met the test of fidelity that is demanded of every son when he said, at the moment of his greatest temptation, "Let it be as you, not I, would have it" (Matthew 26, 39).

4

HUMAN LOVE

Learning to love another human being is the greatest challenge in human experience because it makes the most fundamental moral and psychological demands. Loving another person challenges our most deeply-rooted tendencies toward spiritual and psychological narcissism. Love raises concern for others onto an equal plane with concern for ourselves. And as a man's relations with others deepen, he comes to see that all phases of his loving constitute a single experience, whether the loved one be friend, spouse, child, or God. Here, as psychotheology views it, it is especially true for man to allow no separation between the moral and psychological demands love makes. Every kind of contact furnishes men with more meaningful exercises in the relational activity we call love.

The Analogous Character of Love

Religion and psychology may seem to call forth the exercise of love for differing if not different reasons. In the New Testament we are reminded again and again that the love of man is an absolute prerequisite for the love of God. St. John says, typically, "Anyone who claims to be in the light but hates his brother is still in the dark. But anyone who loves his brother is living in light and need not be afraid of stumbling, unlike the man who hates his brother and is in the darkness, not knowing where he is going because it is too dark to see" (1 John 2, 9-11). But today we are beginning to grasp that the Christian exhortation to love must consider the important underlying psychic factors involved. In the past the main threat to morality and religion seemed to be atheism. For 20th-century man *apersonalism* is far worse, for we have come to see that hatred for another person clearly manifests a denial of transcendent values. A social vision corrupted by hatred, war, and greed can make guilty bedfellows of theist and atheist alike. Religion and psychology both continue to emphasize this in their own way and to offer differing solutions. Humanists recommend a more sensitive awareness of the needs of other men; moralists urge belief in God as the fundamental way of restoring moral sense. But in a psychotheological context both are ultimately confounded by a Christ who speaks of the love of God and man as a single experience. That is why the encounters between man and God and man and man, however different in degree, are analogous. Christianity maintains that there is nothing arbitrary in the command to believe in and love God; but this necessity must also be reflected in the experience we call human love. The poet W. H. Auden says, "We must love one another or die."

Religious tradition holds that what we call the love of God and the love of man are not strictly speaking the same thing because God, as an object of love, is infinitely more worthy. Psychologically, however, this tells us little about the nature of love as an *experience*. Indeed, too often it serves as an excuse. For it is experience which tells us that the love of another human being is infinitely more difficult than the love of God which makes few practical demands if it is viewed (as it often is) as something outside the range of experience. To love another, God or man, is a single operation based upon a single psychodynamic principle — seeing the other as worthy of love. Everything short of this reduces the love experience to the arbitrary, robs it of its power. Even the most well-intentioned person can thus view another man's misery as merely an "occasion" for love, when it must be seen as the only opportunity we have of giving psychological depth to our moral sense. Love, whether of God or man, is a single therapeutic power; it has a single function.

Resistances to Love

The school of "interpersonal psychoanalysis" founded by Harry Stack Sullivan and enriched by Erich Fromm and Karen Horney reveals that anxiety is often a result of distorted relationships with authority figures. In some way the parent, whose role is to lead the uninitiated into meaningful relationships, managed by his own neurotic behavior to impose limited notions of what future relationships would involve. Anyone whose role it is to foster trust in the life of another can just as easily be responsible for causing an imbalance in relationships. Every parent attempts to introduce his child to his own ideal of a cultural spectrum, but there is never any guarantee of the result.

The belief that human relationships are ideal signs of man's relationship to God is the most important psychosocial factor in the Judeo-Christian tradition. Presumably this principle still underlies every experience of personal love. We can trace the sacralization of all human relationships to it. When a man recognizes himself in others, he strengthens the bond which is at one and the same time both morally and psychically vital for the preservation of society.

For the Christian the question is all the more complex, for he claims to see it not merely as a relationship to a far-off divine power, but to the person of Christ himself who, as we saw previously, serves as a "bridge" between divine and human. How is it then that Christians can reach out to participate in what is meant to be a personal dynamic relationship and yet settle for an abstract notion? In our time, the answer to such a question has become especially urgent, for we have come to realize that we cannot relate to a concept of Christ which is outside the range of our relations with human beings. In the past we have tended to view Christ's command that we give "a cup of water in his name" as a work of supererogation. Now we have learned to see that morality can never be a gesture to entice the gods. The factors involved in the psychodynamic act of caring require human intentions that demand expression and that give man a clarity of motive he could not otherwise find. Caring restores a fullness thought impossible, and it opens up untold possibilities for union. In fact it is necessary for survival. Thus, the Christian concept of love takes on a psychological validity only as we comprehend that the moral power of the words of the New Testament is indispensable for the painful task of transforming other human beings into members of one's own life, and a necessary prelude for Christ's vision of universal brotherhood.

The attempt to love others may often be abortive. Often, in our attempt to make our relationships "work out," we are immaturely or even immorally motivated. Moralists may not see much value in such activity, but attempts are at least a beginning. Whenever a man searches for something that transcends the obvious in human relationships, he is at least trying to increase his awareness of what love is. There is an ontology of hope underlying every attempt at communication, even when it is characterized by a limited awareness of what love is. It is this beginning of a sense of relatedness which must be held onto at all costs; it can be sacralized. To love means to love under any and all circumstances. But if we demean the importance of misguided attempts, we fail to witness the universal implications of Christ's command to love. The universal call to love can never be divorced from the personal sense of involvement. Even so "pantheistic" a religion as Buddhism holds that cosmic love must include a sense of personal involvement. A typical passage from the *Sutta-Nipata* illustrates this beautifully: "Just as with her own life a mother shields from hurt her own, her only, child, so let an all-embracing thought for all that lives be thine — an all-embracing love for the universe in all its heights and depths and breadth, unstinted love, unmarred by hate within, not rousing enmity." And these words emanate from a religion Westerners often dismiss as tinged with more than its share of moral sentimentality.

The divine is always celebrated through the encounter of personal love because love always enlightens what is hidden and mysterious; it extends aspirations so that diverse and even discordant elements can be reconciled. St. Paul, addressing the young Christian community, said: "You have stripped off your old behavior with your old self, and you have put on a new self which will progress toward true knowledge the more it is renewed in the image of its creator; and in that image there is no room for distinction between Greek and Jew, between the circumcised and uncircumcised, or between barbarian and Scythian, slave and free man. There is only one Christ; he is everything and he is in everything" (Colossians 3, 9-11). This universal vision must always be the basis of even the most personal emotional involvement.

A man grows morally and psychologically insofar as he is able to strike a balance between personal and universal love. Both theology and psychology tell us little about love when they structure rules for its exercises. Christ's attitude is clearly reflected in what he told the rationalists of his own day. The Pharisees were a priestly class, learned in dogma and rational argument. Because of this Christ often pointed out how difficult it would be for them to understand his new vision of love. It was Christ's advance beyond tribalism that opened a new psychological direction, viewing personal love in cosmic terms.

Christ's contemporaries are like the dogmatists of our own day who find the "sacredness" of humanity merely sentimental. People resist the universally redemptive power of love when they resist the idea of the transcendent in the human. The act of sharing is inhibited by those who see themselves and others as finite. Psychological frustration occurs because men hem themselves in by imaginary boundaries under the guise of being "realistic" and "practical."

That man can so resist his profound need for love is a fact that both moralists and psychologists recognize as the cause of most anti-social and immoral behavior. We say that the resistance flows from an unnatural separation of love into divine and human compartments. By seeing the love of God and man as analogous, we become aware that a man's moral sense grows only as he becomes convinced of the psychic need for human relationships. The realization that love can be found only in the experience of human encounter inevitably provokes resistance and challenge. It may even become a threat when one realizes that it is not only possible but absolutely necessary for an authentic life.

Yet man can move toward a vision of a love which is universal in its scope. Today the distilled essence of Christ's message is becoming increasingly important — in large part, no doubt, because of the psychological revolution. A man who has learned to release himself from his own bondage is in a much better position to love than the man still trapped in emotional self-isolation. For the modern believer, psychological insight has given a deeper dimension to Christ's call to universal love.

Group dynamics, for example, works on the principle that love is a phenomenological experience. Such diverse activities as family therapy, labor-management relations, urban renewal and cultural dialogue have brought the fruits of the psychoanalytic consultation room into a social arena. If the translation into moral and social concern has been slow, it may be due to sensible caution; more often, however, it is the result of pharisaism which inhibits all human enrichment. But the insights of psychology, in conjunction with the Christian command to universal love, are the only answer in our time to a tangled social system.

Experiments in group dynamics have taught us much about the reality of man's desire for reconciliation. In group therapy, change comes about precisely because people are exposed to each other, many for the first time, on an experiential basis. There are no pre-conceptions about "fraternal charity" or "good behavior." Savage hostilities and primitive notions of isolation are brought into a miniature social milieu, where people are encouraged to reach beyond mere social or moral etiquette. Honesty is necessary if one wants to be able to take the consequences of one's own feelings and reactions. This leads to a deepening introspection of motives and the beginnings of psychospiritual honesty.

For some persons, the multiplicity of experiences in therapy may serve as a first opportunity for a familial experience; it allows an assessment of the importance of diversity within the human condition. It points to a basis for comparing mutual emotional responses. Most importantly, when diversity is truly understood as a creative challenge and not merely as a threat, rapport takes on an experiential validity. Unpretending and often blunt statements can often afford people their first chance of becoming directly engaged with another. Candor can expose festering areas of resentments, but even more it can create mutual love and self-esteem. Thus a man can take his first important step out of solitude. Experience with another has allowed him to move from a state where he believed there could be no relationships to a sense of genuine interdependence. There has been a change from distrust to concern.

Experiments in group dynamics justify our radical emphasis on the identity of the experience of divine and human love. Authenticity depends upon a willingness to see the relevance of all human aspirations in reference to a transcendent moral goal — but only through a deepening of psychological rapport. Relational morality is achieved only after people have grasped the psychological constituents of the act of sharing. Sharing requires a recognition of a common denominator among men, and that implies equality. This demands above all that we believe other men are as capable of giving as ourselves, that a genuinely new moral sensitivity can be achieved which takes us far beyond what we are now capable of. Maybe we should stop praying *for* each other and start praying *to* each other.

It is precisely because our age is deeply involved in attempts at reconciliation that it is characterized by upheavals. Our confusion and tension are sure indications that we are searching for a newly structured morality which must take more account of psychological discovery. Traditional morality in our society has been at one and the same time enlightened and tempered by the fact that our unconscious and conscious desires are not always in tune with each other, that our conception of things is not always equivalent to our experience of them.

There are many ways in which this has become manifest. We are coming to learn that the resentments we feel toward each other are no longer easily classifiable as simply moral or immoral, but reflect needs that we ourselves may not yet understand. The hostilities we experience every day of our lives, in important as well as inconsequential ways, indicate in what new ways we are reassessing our moral and psychological behavior.

People abuse each other when they cannot cope with their own anxieties. For example, a man who searches out new and different sexual partners, whenever he can't face the ultimate obligation of human encounter, projects all his fantasies on temporary love objects, rarely giving the persons loved a chance to achieve a reality. Such people are often looking for release from the familiar world which they feel is plaguing them with its demands. They are afraid to deal with the people in their lives — especially the important people — in any meaningful way, because of their dread of being used and perhaps swallowed up. Such people demand heroic moral generosity of themselves while being unable (psychologically) to give it. Escape into a fantasy world becomes the only alternative to one who fails to synchronize his moral and psychological yearnings.

But there are other, more subtle, ways in which we reveal our lack of love for others. We can reduce others to a position of insignificance even when we think we are treating them well. Many liberal whites in American society today, for example, while priding themselves on being non-racist, speak of "giving" minority groups their rights, while at the same time they presume to offer themselves to blacks as examples of civilized morality. This reflects the most offensive kind of paternalism; it denies the very heart of the evangelical message that each person is sacred. The individual experience of grace, seen as psychomoral power, is precisely what gives every man both the right and the obligation to foster social justice. This often takes a great deal of psychological readjustment on the part of those who consider themselves morally motivated because it demands a vision of social justice that incorporates both the moral concept of freedom as a God-given birthright and the idea that men see one another as more than objects. The question of civil rights and the ability of men to see each other as worthy obviously will not be answered by any political panacea; rather, it requires the deepest moral and psychological strength we can muster. In reality it demands a new morality firmly based on psychological honesty.

Moral leadership does not go far enough even when it attempts to transform the human rights struggle into a Christian crusade. It is far more important that Christians should sharpen their own moral sense by a deeper psychological understanding of the social needs of others, in order to find ways of turning "regard" for others into a psychospiritual commandment and to furnish Christian morality with a newer and ever widening basis for the dialogue between the have's and the have-not's.

No matter how psychosocial aberrations reveal themselves, the important fact is that men continue to be at odds with each other only because they have been unable to effect relationships of any moral and psychological worth. But social aberrations at least reflect the struggle men make to become part of an acceptable reality. For those who focus exclusively on the present moment, immediate enthusiasms provide release in promiscuous sex, or even violence. And to recognize the needs, however frustrated and distorted they have become, is to begin to sacramentalize them. The deepest longings of even the most anxious and restless members of society can be given new moral and psychological significance.

Psychotheological emphasis goes to the heart of the problem of human relations in its insistence that love can become viable when men are willing to see the essential relevance of *all* human aspirations. It is only when men strip each other of those aspirations that they are kept from mutual concern and love.

Developmental psychology demonstrates that the beginning of resistance to love can be traced to parental deprivation, actual or imagined. For a psychotic it may lead to bizarre symptoms divorced from reality because of tragedies in early life. The impulse to love and to be loved is realized only with difficulty in the life of a person who does not carry the memory of love from the beginnings of conscious life. Religion has come to see that even the noblest moral exhortations cannot overcome a chronic sense of alienation and the desperate quality a man's yearnings can take as he grows older.

The most common resistance stems from a refusal to accept the presence and value of diversity. Many men refuse to accept the simple fact that we live in a world of diverse interests and needs, a "multiverse," to use William James' expression. Experience cannot be tailored to fit individual needs alone. It is true that a man who continues to live stubbornly within his own limited boundaries does so because of social and cultural conditioning; he is bound by the legacy of his inheritance, and he finds the sharing of another's vision difficult, if not impossible. But the true barriers to communication that we experience are not due to cultural diversity. They are a reflection of cultural prejudices and false hopes. Anthropologists have shown that tribal taboos can very easily determine a man's life-style. Studies in psychology have further shown that even sense perception can reveal social unbalance. The size of a small coin may appear enormous to a slum child, yet unexceptionally normal to a child who has no sense of being deprived.

Diversity is never evil, unless, of course, it leads to conflict. The great English poet William Blake, in one of those pre-psychiatric insights for which he has become famous, says:

> The vision of Christ that thou dost see
> Is my vision's greatest enemy.
> Thine has a great hook nose like thine,
> Mine has a snub nose like to mine.
> Thine is the friend of all Mankind;
> Mine speaks in parables to the blind.
> Thine loves the same world that mine hates;
> Thy heaven doors are my hell gates.

Perhaps it takes the intuition of a poet to see diversity in such a positive light. The desire to wish diversity away, for both religious and psychological reasons, can lead only to an intensification of human estrangement. To see it as part and parcel of psychospiritual maturity is the first step in overcoming the barriers that separate men. It is distorted vision, not a sense of diversity, which sets men at odds with each other.

Depressive and Expressive Love

Many of the anxieties we feel about human relationships are due to limited notions of our emotional responses. Perhaps the most difficult to overcome is the romantic notion that human communication inevitably includes pain, loneliness and frustration. It is true that while love promises satisfaction and union, it almost always involves other reactions. The characteristic poses of depression are many, and are expressed by most people in terms of feelings of being abandoned, maltreated, or misunderstood. But for all the reality of the pain, it can be said that depression of this type is almost always an escape. It is even an indication of what price one is willing to pay to remain unrelated. It is of little value when used as a neurotic stance to justify one's self-willed helplessness. From a psychotheological vantage point — where hope is as much a sign of health as it is a moral virtue — even pain must have a valid role to play.

This is not to imply that the opposite of depression is to be sought in a sense of elation or in some thrill that would serve as an antidote for the pain of alienation. Rather, the solution can be found in a sense of *expression,* a coming alive, a learning to respond, to take risks, when one finds oneself capable of making real commitments to others. To be expressive is to recognize one's expansiveness, in contrast to the self-constriction of depression. This, too, carries something of a price tag to the unwary. Pain is as much an accompaniment of the outgoing individual as it is of the introvert. But always it is the *quality* of the pain that is important. One who engages in life welcomes all the pain inherent in human relationships. The choice, in other words, is to take either a depressive stand which inhibits relationships or an expressive position which keeps one continually open to what new encounters may come one's way.

The depressive stance always accentuates the fear of loss. Yet mature relationships never end. Long after friends cease seeing one another, they continue to live out the influence that their friendship has had. The twinges of pain that besiege us when we think back on some past relationship should lead to a renewal of present alliances, not to wistful remorse or cynical withdrawal. Even the recollection of a dead parent or friend takes on a therapeutic power for enhancing a sense of relatedness to the living. The memory of dead persons has a real bearing on present relationships. For many people it becomes necessary to make the dead present in order to forgive them. Religion, too, for its own reasons, advocates praying to or for one's dead.

What Christians call their relationship to Christ can be seen in this light. Like any relationship this one is psychologically alive only in the sense that its dynamism can influence man's present relationships. Love for another person, whether dead or alive, must always be an expressive project. This is what the command "to love one another as he loved us" clearly implies. Some persons have always found it strategically impossible to follow this command. Indeed, most Christians could write their autobiographies as the story of attempts to accept the command intellectually while remaining paralyzed by prejudices and shortsightedness. But the Christ-relationship is meaningful only to the person who literally wants to make Christ alive again, who brings Christ back from the dead.

What religion speaks of as "grace," the power that gives man the ability to overcome spiritual anxiety, can be resisted as easily as man resists psychic helps. Possessiveness, greed, envy are all blocks to man's moral and psychological instincts. From a psychomoral point of view, these are perversions, weapons of a self-destructive, depressive stance; they can be overcome only by healing through a religious therapy and psychological therapy which share a common purpose.

Religion and psychotherapy encourage committed engagement with life. Both can be distorted to emphasize a kind of pulling back in order to insure personal safety. Insofar as they foster openness, they become true protectors of the role that love can play in cementing human relationships, and, consequently, the reconciliation of society. The establishment of relationships is the first step in establishing any community. As a stranger becomes familiar, we are in a better position to reach out to him to join our lives more closely. Our differences will never disappear; we will find it necessary to sacrifice a degree of autonomy. Total autonomy, in fact, is a psychospiritual fantasy which prevents us from opening ourselves to a larger reality.

Man's fulfillment comes through relationships. If in the past theology has insisted that paradise could be won only by making sacrifices for the good of one's soul, modern man has translated that sense of sacrifice to a level where the suppression of autonomy has the single, honest purpose of participating more profoundly in the greater good of all of humanity.

Love and Anxiety

The instinct to resolve the sense of separateness from other human beings is fraught with danger, for even when expressed in desire for communion it seems to be accompanied by some form of anxiety. But when this desire is carried beyond the limits of emotional balance it begins to express itself in anxieties of the worst type: fear of loss, jealousy, or even both.

A certain necessary asceticism must accompany human relationships. It is as sound psychologically as spiritually. It was spoken of by St. Paul when he exhorted: "When Christ freed us, he meant us to remain free. Stand firm, therefore, and do not submit again to the yoke of slavery" (Galatians 13, 1). The free man will not panic at fear of loss. He enriches his relationships by a liberty that lets him function fully, unconstrained by fear of loss. His zest for life allows him confrontation, not domination. In still another letter Paul described the freedom he had achieved through maturity in Christ: "I know how to be poor and I know how to be rich, too. I have been through my initiation and now I am ready for anything anywhere: full stomach or empty stomach, poverty or plenty" (Philippians 4, 12). Freedom is the mainstay of a mature lifestyle. Real comradeship — whether friendship, parenthood or marriage — can thrive only by the intention of not holding the other as if he were an object. Neither God nor man can exist if he must be owned in order to be.

The beginning of a mature social sense is determined in infancy. A child looks for people and objects to reassure him. It is not until he gradually comes to terms with the fact that he is surrounded by people who have their own special needs that he can begin his quest for inter-personal relationships. This begins through the mother-child relationship but is by no means limited to it. The father plays a strong role here, since he too vies for the mother's affection. Excessive emphasis on the Freudian notion of the oedipal conflict ignores the growing desire on the part of a child to want to please his father, not merely appease him. Early relationships with friends, brothers and sisters, even pets, all serve as inspirations to the growing child, as models of others who call forth a sense of concern.

The birth of social sense should find a parallel expression in the religious experience. Religious practice seems to have forgotten the importance of the social initiation of the infant. Baptism, for example, has become more and more a ritual and less an experience. Emphasis has been put on the "cleansing" power of baptism, washing the infant of the stain of "original sin." But the truer symbolism, and one which is gradually being restored, is that it opens the door to a sense of shared environment. Water, the simplest symbol, is more than a cleansing agent; it symbolizes the fluidity of life itself, the introduction to a spiritual ambience where involvement and brotherhood become a common experience. Baptism, like any other ritual, has too often tended to play a divisive, fragmenting role in the community. There is always a tendency to reject it on the grounds that it would separate us from, rather than join us to, the mass of mankind. Thus, in a psychotheological sense, the refusal to be baptized can be a truer baptism when it shows us how we can overcome the anxieties that keep us from each other.

Anxiety can be made to play a positive role when it informs the deeper self that the search for love is a never-ending one. This form of anxiety must exclude destructive and infantile tendencies in order to be sublimated to what can be called a level of "excitement." It understands that confrontation can be fruitful only under certain conditions. It starts by acknowledging man's dread of the nothingness which preceded his individual existence and the existence of the human species. But it also involves a realization that the forces of evolution and salvation did have a beginning, and from that moment and through all subsequent moments man has a destiny.

Beneficial anxiety eventually lifts a man above the infantile, where interpersonal relations take on sacramental dimensions. Life becomes an experience of freedom shared with others. Man becomes aware that he can attain the flexibility which dispels all *confining* anxiety. Love thus becomes a psychomoral force; and the absence of love is not merely the end of growth, but conflict and death — moral, emotional and psychological. On a religious level, the Christian who, as St. Paul says, considers himself "to be dead to sin but alive for God in Christ Jesus" (Romans 6, 11) has sensed that participating in the forces of survival means living a life of grace. Progress becomes the continual unfolding of every man's salvation and ultimate redemptive hope. To be alive thus means to be alive to the heart of evolution; to open oneself to the graces of love is to shun death.

The sacredness of the human community always begins with this affirmation of love and freedom, even at great personal risk. A social system remains morally and psychologically healthy only as it fosters and protects healthy, personal relationships and frees man from the enslavement of racism, war, economic injustice — anything that fosters a sense of personal futility.

All constructive communal organisms, be they churches or governments, have the opportunity to create the necessary foundations for social and personal evolution. Deeper undercurrents of family and friendship are arrived at only after man transcends the pose of personal solitude. Psychotheology sees this as the primary obligation of any institution which claims, as do democracy and Christianity, to be involved in the causes of human freedom and justice. The mature person accepts his role in building the earth: "This is the commandment which you have heard since the beginning, to live a *life of love*" (2 John 1, 6).

The expectation of universal love is no impossible dream. It is based on an evolving optimism derived from the very structure of experience and life itself which sees that God and man are advocates of each other, and that this mutual relationship is mirrored in the interrelatedness of men themselves. Experience tells us that we become more authentic and alive as our sense of reconciliation with everything grows. Even the differences between men enrich our common life. Human wills may clash, even bloodily, but for the man of faith, even this bears witness to an intrinsic relationship, however perverted, of those in conflict. Men are members of one community even if it is only the pitifully limited community of mutual distrust or hatred.

Trust begets further trust. With the initial stirrings of trust comes the courage to accept the risks inherent in saying "yes" to the world, to men, to God. A mature sense of trust finally frees man to explore the feeling that he does have a measure of control over the chaotic forces within himself and society. This germ of trust requires much nurturing; but as a man learns to look into the hearts of others and to sense a mutual need for reconciliation, he begins to have confidence that such a goal can be achieved — but only when love is seen as a psychic as well as a religious power.

5

IDENTITY

Both religion and psychology are concerned with personality development and stress the importance of the quest for identity. The sacrament of baptism, for example, by bestowing a name, stamps the person as an individual. Psychotheology would deepen the meaning of this ritual. We are prepared to say that God himself can become personalized in human consciousness as each person comes to a greater awareness of self.

Identity and Redemption

As we have seen, Incarnation makes the unity of mankind clearer as men grow in consciousness. Another way of saying this is that all men share in the one identity we call humanity, and the fulfillment of this identity is in the person of Christ. In him we see laid to rest for all time the notion that man is by nature separate from God. The history of Christianity can be read as the process whereby men gradually abandon a sense of isolation and self-importance and see themselves as a democratic whole by sharing in the identity of the power we call God. To the degree that we fail, we abandon our right to be called Christians. Yet even our failures do not preclude the appearance and reappearance of the power of Christ as the living link that unites us all. We are like the loaves and fishes which were distributed on the hills near the Sea of Galilee: our human identities may be multiplied, but we all come from a single hand.

Christ never made the fulfillment of individual personality contingent upon some future salvation. Redemption comes in the here and now as we engage more deeply in the business we call life. That is why sermons about heaven often leave people in a land of fantasy and have little psychological worth. Man can never seek personal redemption apart from his environment. Psychotheology is concerned with man as a dynamic entity, but only within his present cultural experience. Here the traces of his childhood together with his adult maturity shape his personality. Yet it is not difficult to see why people continue to have problems in coming to terms with their environment. Christ pointed out the difficulty people have in recognizing their prophets, for the prophet's task has always been to remind men that they must come alive to the Christ in their midst, that they must constantly transform what appears to be merely natural into more than its apparent worth. Religion views this transformation as conversion and the search for moral perfection; we would say it is the need to recognize personal experience of one's environment as continually redeemable. A man who loses faith in his environment loses his identity as the offspring of the creative principle we call God.

Neurotics cannot stand themselves or other people. They have literally become allergic to themselves and live on pretenses. This usually comes out in the form of self-hatred. Even their continual yearning for reassurance comes to naught since ultimately they believe no one. In a psychotheological sense, *the neurotic represents the unredeemed*. He has lost faith in his own potential. He feels orphaned and tends to see the world as a thing to be manipulated rather than as a place where he is free to develop his own experience. He may even resort to violence, since he has no real regard for his own views and therefore cannot see others as anything more than puppets who either bend to his wishes or continually fail him. This violence may turn outward or inward, as, for example, in psychosomatic illness or debilitating anxiety.

True psychological health may be defined as a process in which the balance between the neurotic and healthy tilts in favor of the healthy. In psychotheological terms, the non-neurotic portion of the personality redeems the neurotic portion. This dialectic between progressive and reactionary forces takes place within each person. Discovery of identity is precisely the coming alive to one's resources. Each individual — each community — constantly gropes for an identity, and it is this search that constitutes what religious instinct calls the need for redemption.

Neurosis may be compared to the fall from grace. It would be easy to push the comparison too far, however. Even in a psycho-theological context they are not precisely the same thing. A person who suffers psychic pain because of early conditioning in childhood cannot be put into the same category as a person who willfully uses evil to achieve his own gains. It would be incorrect to equate sin and neurosis.

Yet psychotheology sees the possibility of relating the two in a new frame of reference, attempting to avoid rigid definitions. We insist that people seek identity — identity that is dynamic. Each person must emerge from a static notion of himself. Since psycho-theology is non-categorical, non-diagnostic, we acknowledge that each person has, as a part of his life-style, a dynamic mixture of evolutionary qualities and retrogressive "security blankets" which manifest themselves in rigidity and fear. Redemption thus becomes both a psychological and spiritual activity, for the redemptive process is a search for emotional and spiritual wholeness.

The book of Revelation viewed Christ as "*the first* and *the last,* who was dead and has come to life again*" (Revelation 2, 8). Later it says of those who are willing to cast their lot with the redemptive process, who wish to ally themselves with Christ: "To those who prove victorious I will give the hidden manna and a white stone — a stone with a *new name* written on it, known only to the man who receives it" (Revelation 2, 17). The hidden name is the ego striving to assert its right to be. This is achieved as a person plunges into the perpetual death and resurrection that engages him every day of his life. "Engagement" implies being part of life rather than acting as a spectator. A person receives his identity as the result of urging himself on to a new birth in mental and moral pursuits. Sin and mental anguish have an important role to play in this process; both may be traced to a frustrated desire for meaning. The quest for identity has many false starts, but every action taken is *experience;* there is no waste. Man yearns essentially for a whole identity, and in this search he meets forces in himself, some for which he is responsible and some not. Some are truly redemptive, bringing emotional expressiveness and moral nourishment; others may aim at the same goals but lack strong foundations. Jeremiah forecast "doom for the man who founds his palace on anything but integrity" (Jeremiah 22, 13). Likewise, Paul in one of his letters stated: "You must be rooted in him [Christ] and built to him and held firm by the faith you have been taught" (Colossians 2, 7). A psychological parallel to both statements may be seen in the acknowledgment that psychotherapists give to the need for a loving and secure childhood. Anything less will have to be counteracted by corrective emotional therapy. For a religious man, atonement for sins is an advance toward sanctity. For a man who stumbles in his search for psychic growth there is the possibility of reeducation through psychotherapy or other means, in order to learn alternatives to neurotic behavior. In both cases we see man's *single* quest for identity.

It is not easy for anyone to redeem himself. The battle rages between an emerging self and regressive parts of the personality. Most personalities are weighed down with protective devices — what the psychoanalyst calls "defenses." People try to ward off threats to their status quo, and sometimes this armor insures the individual against undue anxiety. It shields the personality much as an antibody protects the physical organism from infections. Still, there are times when inflammations and fevers used by the antibodies as instruments of protection get out of control. So, too, the psychic and moral defenses may backfire and prevent renewal from taking place. Regressive forces, psychological and spiritual, unite with the very defenses which were meant to insure the individual's emotional survival. Such defenses encourage fear, panic, bigotry, idolatry, violence and destructiveness and provide the person with a temporary false identity.

Like Christ, no man need run from commitments to love and renewal. Only in this way can man become open to the future. He can accept the many phases of his life. It will not be necessary for him to clutch at morbid memories of his childhood and youth. He can pursue his life without constantly looking back. He can leave the security of the categorical and pre-digested and yet feel secure that he is involved in the dynamic process of living.

Finding one's identity requires a kind of relaxed security which prevails even in times of disappointment. Christ understood who he was even while he suffered humiliation and violence. Jacob became aware of himself through his mission. He had falsified his appearance to Isaac, his father, to get the birthright of the firstborn so that he could become a patriarch to his people. Jacob wrestled with God and insisted on a new name. The new name was "Israel," the sign and seal of his true identity.

Men may seek out new names in order to become closer to the truth about themselves. Spinoza changed his name from Baruch to Benedict because he felt it better expressed his sense of himself. This was a common practice from the time of the Middle Ages, and until recently it was adopted by religious as a way of expressing their ideals. Nowadays, too, blacks have taken to renaming themselves as a sign that they are no longer tied to the time when their ancestors were slaves and adopted the names of their white masters. In this way they have come to assert themselves before the world.

But all are ultimately reduced to the one name — man — since through all diversity something intrinsic is expressed. The primogeniture of Adam can be understood psychotheologically as the man each person is. Whether or not mankind had a single set of parents is beside the point; the point is that man has the psychological and spiritual ability to relate to and communicate with other men. Only as he makes use of this basic identity can he be said to rise beyond his limits.

Christ as Universal Identity

The contemporary media explosion reduces the cultural differences between peoples, making it imperative to communicate in ways that will lead to mutual understanding. Television screens and cables, among other things, are the vascular systems of the community of mankind. Just as the names of each person form a mosaic that is his identity, so the community is a larger mosaic called mankind. Christ, or the new Adam, personifies the complete identity of mankind. If Christ is represented by his Church, then the Church cannot be narrow and sectarian. Anything less indicates the presence of the anti-Christ, since it excludes, at least in theory, some men from their birthright, and no person or institution has the right to do that. Laws or customs based on fear exclude Christ, even though they may have been intended to protect the community from the anti-Christ. We can see this in the case of saints who were martyred by the "official" representatives of Christ. The idea of many mansions in heaven implies that there are many roads to heaven. Whenever Christ is anything less than the universal identity, incorporating all names, to that extent he is obscured by the forces of reaction.

Psychotheology sees Christ as the basis of a universal consciousness. He shared mankind's life, allowing men to be in intimate communion with God. Christian morality must therefore be universal, since Christ did not preach a tribal god. Nevertheless, he was introduced to the world as a man from a traditional culture. He emerged from the rich heritage of the Hebrew people but he transcended his community because, as he told the Pharisees, "I know where I came from and where I am going." His community was more extensive than any of its natives could see. Their fear of the universal blinded their vision and made them suspicious of anything or anyone who was extraordinary. Continuing his discussion with the Pharisees, Jesus said, "You do not know where I come from or where I am going. You judge by human standards; I judge no one" (John 8, 14-15).

The psychotheological implications of this state of mind are important. Christ never renounced his community; rather, he *extended* it. In other words he was not provincial. He did not subject himself to the narrow prejudices and taboos of his clan. Had he identified with those attitudes, he never could have had the insights and sensitivity of universal Savior. He did not curse his native land, but neither was he a stranger to all nations. He simply was a man who renounced narrowness because he saw life in cosmic terms. Today, likewise, his ministry is fulfilled only by those who have gone beyond nationalism and sectarianism. Invariably they are found among the peacemakers and others who put mankind's search above national interest.

A universal identity presupposes the notion of a source. Jung developed Freud's theory of the personal unconscious in terms of a "collective unconscious," indicating that the human family is not necessarily time-bound or space-bound. Each man draws his inspiration and creative impetus from this model. According to Jung, each individual carries within him the entire history of mankind and draws from it as he tries to individuate himself. From a psychotheological standpoint, it might be postulated not merely that Christ is universal consciousness, but also that the God whom we and he call "Father" is universal unconsciousness. The individuation of God takes place through Christ in us. This by no means turns God or Christ into impersonal principles. Nor does it negate the intimacy man derives from communion with the divine. Quite the opposite: Christ, representing the archetype of universal consciousness, becomes radically present to people who unify their lives with his moral vision. At the same time there is a growing awareness of an infused divinity or evolutional unconscious which unites man with purposiveness and transcendent destiny. When man prays he addresses the God who has already given him the strength to go on. His identity is affirmed by his having kept faith with his own capacities. Psychoanalysis tries to show man how his conditioning has kept him from becoming part of the mainstream of life. It opens him to many possibilities once he loosens the bonds of psychic infancy. It follows, in a psychotheological frame of reference, that men may repress the universal aspiration which is God because they fear to let go of their established concepts of life. Once man allows himself the freedom from psychological and moral impairment, he is free to release more of himself, which ultimately spells out more fully the universal identity of mankind itself.

The unconscious in each man therefore becomes elaborated in consciousness only when certain rigid barriers are removed. The unconscious part of man is baptized just as surely as the conscious.

Christ's life made the reality of this baptism clear, but the immediate impact on his life can continue to have meaning only as men evolve to a point where they can get beyond defensiveness. This liberation allows for union with the power of God. Christ is the liberator in the sense that he consciously exemplified the message of the universal unconscious — that all men arise from the same source. To kill or inflict harm on another would be suicide. Mankind persists in murdering itself, but the risen Christ is the external reappearance of consciousness proclaiming that despite self-inflicted destruction, an eternal principle of renewal perpetually comes forth. Each person is an affirmation of the presence of life. Like Christ, he transcends the temporal.

Men have always sensed, as Plato so beautifully suggested, that there must be some mode of pre-existence. The psychotheological interpretation of this intuition is that man has always existed in the mind of God. No man comes into the world as a *tabula rasa*. He is in a real sense fully prepared from the first moment to continue the universal process. The community redeems the individual by letting him contribute to the universal continuum. Man's common origin is his only guide. His love strengthens the close weave of creation; his hatred unravels it.

In order to transcend narrowness, an individual must examine his tendency to clutch others as if they were possessions. A parent who is too strict, a lover constantly agitated by jealousy, a person who has become so dependent on someone else that he feels no identity except through the other, must learn what it means to let go. Such a person is afraid to let go, fearful of being "set adrift." To be freed from his possessiveness, he must relearn what it is to have an identity. People who have matured in this way can participate in the lives of others without treating them like puppets.

The process of reaching for one's identity is exemplified in the experiential process of psychotherapy, a process based on the idea that a person must come to recognize how other people's actions threaten him. Earlier we said that people have a common heritage, and that killing another is no different from killing oneself. But even emotional domination of another, overtly or covertly, is a form of murder, for it denies each individual the right to live, to his own identity. In psychotherapy a person learns how to see himself as an individual and as part of mankind. He experiences giving and receiving from others. He learns that he has the capacity to enrich others and to be enriched by them. Personal identity can be achieved in no other way. Thus modern psychological insight confirms what saints and mystics in the past have always known.

Neurotic possessiveness focuses on competition and the relative worth of one course as opposed to another. Through psychoanalytic practice, insights have been gained which can help people become sufficiently aware of their own identities so as not to envy others. Christ related to men in all walks of life. His associates included learned as well as simple men, tax collectors and prostitutes. Love is reductive. It comes into being as it relates itself to a center. One who recognizes that another expresses this center in some way can allow the other person to be. He need not be judgmental.

Identity and Diversity

An individual is able to appreciate other identities as he comes to see variety in himself. This assortment of feelings provides sufficient reason for him to be sympathetic with many varieties of people. Cultural anthropology proves man's willingness to attune himself to distinctive cultures. The "boundary mentality" will consistently oppose a true recognition that other identities do truly exist.

The cultural anthropologist stresses how mores and traditions which have been considered universal in the past (despite outer trappings) are nevertheless signs of unique modes of living. The spaces between cultures are considered barriers only by people who hold rigid views about human nature. It was this kind of mentality which condoned religious wars and inquisitions. The unbending mind in its insecurity fails to see relationships; it insists on a conformism which denies the existence of more than one type of identity. Anthropological evidence, however, informs us that the image of man cannot be frozen in one absolute mold. To do so would be to make an idol of one particular adaptation to life.

Other forms of absolutism having to do with ideal identity rob people of their reference point to God as dynamic mystery. St. Paul preached that "the God who made the world and everything in it . . . does not make his home in shrines made by human hands" (Acts 17, 24). In psychotheological terminology this statement indicates that no attempt to project a static image of man onto the power we call God can ever succeed. Projection is that tendency to remain fixed within oneself, never admitting that the other can be anything but what one is oneself. It is a denial of relationship, since in order to mature both morally and psychologically one must become open to variety in life.

St. Paul further teaches that God "created the whole human race so they could occupy the entire earth, but he decreed how long each nation should flourish and what the boundaries of its territory should be" (Acts 17, 26). He did this so all nations could advance on their own spiritual journey "by feeling their way toward him [and thus] succeed in finding him." In other words, no experience can be dismissed as inauthentic. No one person or nation has the right to invade the sacred boundaries of individual identity and dignity. Further, the tendency to subvert another's identity indicates a severe psychological defect and enormously detracts from the possibility of developing a genuine relationship.

Cultural anthropology makes man understandable without depriving him of his identity. In fact, it emphasizes — just as strongly as the tablets delivered by Moses to the children of Israel — that the chief sin is idolatry. Individuals have no right to see themselves and the culture they happen to belong to as the "absolute" standard for the rest of mankind. The need for God is obvious, since he is the identity which transcends any attempt at categorization and which includes an infinite variety of possibilities which claim for him the right to be Lord of all. Any attempt to attribute this universality to a "select" group results in still more idol-building.

Every individual has the potential to relate to every other individual. This does not have to mean a dimunition of identity; it is invariably an expansion of it — it acknowledges that universality is the ability to relate, the ability to know what it means to be a friend. This transcendent quality does not result in "angelism" or weak philanthropy, nor does it supplant the cultural identity of the individual. Rather, it is that quality which allows the person to listen and be open. It regards the other as having worth. It represents the fulfillment of the messianic hope expressed in Isaiah 11, 6-8:

> The wolf lives with the lamb,
> the panther lies down with the kid,
> calf and lion cub feed together
> with a little boy to lead them.
> The cow and the bear make friends,
> their young lie down together.
> The lion eats straw like the ox.
> The infant plays over the cobra's hole;
> into the viper's lair
> the young child puts his hand.

This promise is Christian, and therefore human, fulfillment. The "little boy" who leads on is the Christ who dispels the notion that differences must create enemies. The psychotherapist, acting as a mediator between the individual and what the individual considers emotionally threatening, operates as the peacemaker. He does it by approaching his patient with respect and with the knowledge that, even given a private fantasy world, communication is the basic factor in healing. The therapist plunges ahead, using tactics in communication as his instruments. He is not limited to verbal interpretations of behavior. In fact the non-verbal interventions he employs are frequently oriented toward an expression of feeling. The posture which the therapist assumes, the tone of voice he uses, the frequent silences — are all meant to convey a total acceptance of the patient's struggle for identity. Therapeutic goals are rarely directed at remolding the individual in a preordained pattern. Emphasis is ideally placed on helping the patient increase his own self-regard so that he will be open to more possibilities in his life. Only the individual who is self-accepting is in a position to accept others.

This attitude can be seen in Jesus' life. He lived and proclaimed an open standard. He made his point by clarifying the distance between light and darkness, between "above" and "below," implying always that man has the choice to limit his vision or extend it. The dynamic notion of the new birth — "I lay down my life in order to take it up again" — envisions a new strength, a confident identity. "No one takes it away from me; I lay it down of my own free will, and as it is in my power to lay it down, so it is in my power to take it up again" (John 10, 17-18). Christ's new birth *is* his universal identity. The psychotheologian may see it as a new consciousness, an identity which, while acknowledging individual differences and personal boundaries, is yet able to transcend the barriers imposed by narrowness.

Both religious language, which speaks in sacramental symbols and ritual, and psychoanalytic psychology, which expresses itself in scientific terminology, lay claim to the free personality who has an open acceptance of life and other human beings. The focus of this kind of identity is squarely set on an expanded view of relationships. Unfortunately, there have been distortions of this "new man." Nietszche's superman is one who has finally been able to live his life without the need of consolation; this was meant to represent an elevation of personal dignity. Freud found the Nietzschean concept compatible with his idea of the individual who is capable of love and vocational satisfaction. However, when the "superman" concept was bent to the interests of Nazi Germany, it saw the complete perversion of Christian purposes and psychological fulfillment. In the guise of evolution to an advanced variety of man, it mocked the sacredness of human life. The monumental crimes it perpetrated are a gruesome reminder that "advancement" can be used for purposes of evil. Moreover, whatever motivated the Nazi mentality still lives as a genuine threat to the authentic desire for advancement.

Mankind is still tempted to opt for a fascistic response to the demands of community. Man is capable of inflicting the worst indignities on others in the name of advancement. However, the Christian "superman" operates on a different level. As he recognizes the expansion of his spiritual potential, he rids himself of his infantile need for reassurance. More than that, he comes to terms with his own identity, making it possible to reexpress the consciousness Christ exemplified. He *dies* to superficial values and easy consolation of his own "free will" and *becomes alive* to the humanizing adventure of building the world. In effect, he becomes a healer, not so much intentionally as by increasingly saying "yes" to those forces which seem most likely to create a truly democratized community.

The transcendence from bigotry and "self-protection" shows how one personality can help to ameliorate the suffering caused by dehumanizing forces. The great spiritual systems are significant only as they call individuals to participate in the moral evolution of the world. There are many pathways to this goal; it would be idle to dwell on the merits of one direction as opposed to another, since God is the center of all experience. The true believer need not seek a distant goal, since God is everywhere present.

Psychoanalytic inquiry has demonstrated that man lives with many varieties of experience, conscious and unconscious. In this sense his goal is always with him. He seeks to release his possibilities and expose them to his consciousness. Even his social sense will loom large as a part of him (already there) trying to be born. As he brings more of himself to the fore, he relates more fully to others for his self-disclosures enlarge his perception of the identity of the community. There is literally more to humanity the more he becomes alive to himself.

A person who begins to accept his own moral and psychological identity becomes capable of personal direction. His ego shows him the many courses he may pursue with some degree of satisfaction. His increased awareness of his tendencies sets them free, and he learns to appreciate who he is. There are, of course, a multitude of resistances along the way. People become terrified of uncovering their hidden feelings, since most people are suspicious of the tendency to depart from social norms. Underneath the psychological skin there are bound to be fantasies and fears which can be frightening. Psychotherapy frequently goes slowly and with caution here, for patients who undergo treatment are not always prepared to be introduced to new areas of their personalities without preparation. Likewise, mature spiritual teachers at times have to provide their students with a balanced view of sin. Even well-intentioned people easily become scrupulous or overly self-critical upon examination of conscience, especially if they have been out of touch with their feelings. Christ pleaded that there be no judgment or hasty condemnation — not because he considered human beings incapable of equitable verdicts but because he knew that differences in human nature often put people off and prevent them from responding spontaneously.

The fear of the unknown can become projected to the point of attributing threatening characteristics to other people. The frightened individual, unsure about the survival of his ego, wants to protect himself. In his uncertainty and fear he can become narrow-minded; in order to compensate for uncertainty, he makes someone else his whipping-boy. He retreats into a safe haven, taking only a very small part of himself with him. He does not see that it is possible to appreciate the fullness of himself only as he becomes secure enough to face a host of feelings. The psychotheological notion would be that no man must ever condemn himself. He must be "objective" about himself; but psychotheologically this means that the deepening awareness of the psychic factors of his personality will never lead to self-condemnation, but always to self-acceptance.

Psychoanalysis illustrates the part played by the limitless quality of the unconscious in the psychological life of a person. If psycho-theology sees one definition of God as the Great Unconscious who is brought to consciousness by living creatures, then in this sense the process of individuation is the recognition of the infinite in the human psyche. Self-acceptance means being open to all life. It constantly brings into consciousness the creative energies which link man with God. However, this revelation is not instantaneous any more than an infant's nervous system is fully developed at birth. The young person, like the novice in religious development, maintains a kind of freshness which gradual sophistication builds upon. Yet too often people "come to terms" with their youth. They become "solid citizens," and in so doing remove themselves from the openness (albeit awkwardness) of their youth. Their rigidity is not so much a fear of impulses as a renunciation of what they once were. Instead of building on their early idealism and social consciousness, they retreat into a sort of self-imposed isolation and conservatism which pass for wisdom. Just when their idealism could benefit from the full scope of their maturity, they settle for "stability." What they fail to see is that the daily death the bible speaks of is not only a death to sin, but also an acknowledgment that *identity is constantly redeemed by rebirth.* As the author of Hebrews said: "Our one desire is that every one of you should go on showing the same earnestness to the end, to the perfect fulfillment of our hopes" (Hebrews 6, 11). The quality of earnestness characterizes those who keep faith with their whole lives. This means accepting a constantly renewed youthfulness of personality. It does not mean an imitation of youthful fads and fashions but sustaining a curiosity about the world, a desire for increasing autonomy, and a willingness to challenge established mores and customs. It means at least being open to what is renewable in the social system. A person who sees life as a process, building from early aspirations, will have no time for the fears of those who would halt progress toward greater human rights and increased freedom of individual expression.

Christian morality in its most expansive form is based on the maturing process. Seeing life as a process gives priority to experience, no part of which should be excluded from the fullness of life. A human being comes to appreciate his identity as he recognizes his distinct place in the human complex, a place which draws its strength from the central creative power we call God. Each man individuates this creative center by recognizing the basic respect he owes to his life. Repression and rigidity hamper a person's appreciation of his experience.

Psychotheology would formulate the developmental process as that opportunity which we all have (not in equal degree, of course) to come to some understanding with the realities of life. More specifically, however, we see the crisis of faith as paralleling growth and early socialization. For instance, a baby's experience of love and warmth may set the stage for the dimension of experience we call religious faith. If no preparation is given to a youngster to learn to bear his moments of solitude, he will be in a poor position to appreciate his individuality. A child who has learned his lesson well usually comes from a home where he has not been unduly teased or manipulated to satisfy a parent's whim. There has to be some consistency in handling an infant's needs so that he can learn to trust his environment. A parent must recognize the individuality of a child and patiently learn to communicate with him. St. Luke reports that Mary, the mother of Jesus, "treasured all these things [which had been prophesied about her son] and pondered them in her heart." Psychotheologically, every child has his identity prophesied. A parent who shows respect and interest will not miss any essential quality of his child's growing identity. No general ground-rules can ever be made about infant- and child-rearing. Each new life is in a position to communicate and correspond with those who comprise his world. Only the most profound psychological and religious insights instruct parents to regard their child's existence as worthy of total respect.

Psychotheology stresses the reverence which should be granted to all identities. In this way, mankind finds renewed impetus for growth and development. It is hoped that this spontaneity and freshness of children will remain throughout an individual's entire existence; spontaneous leaps are the only signs that life is in process and that a person's identity is constantly deepening. Where it goes can never be firmly predicted. It has infinite possibilities to express the many facets of life in its own style. All men have to become conscious of the many potentials operative in their lives.

To be actualized a person's existence must become understandable. Understanding oneself opens the doors of communication and introduces dialogues with others. Lack of clarity in a person's life is usually the result of some fear that he might be destroyed if truly understood. Likewise, the fear of bringing one's own unconscious to the realm of consciousness is fraught with many reservations resulting in personal repression.

When identity ceases to involve growth and development, it is for all practical purposes dead to itself. "Let your behavior change, modeled by your new mind," St. Paul advises, in telling the early Christians how to seek virtue in constant psychological renewal. "This is the only way to discover the will of God and know what is good, what it is that God wants, what is the perfect thing to do" (Romans 12, 2). We can find no clearer expression of how moral health and psychological health are really, in terms of experience, one and the same thing.

6

TIME

It has been said that the Oriental mind has escaped many of the anxieties of the West, because historically it has been impervious to the meaning and value of time in human experience. But the misunderstanding of time is more than a cultural curiosity; it can be a psychological trap in any culture. Every man carries within himself many temptations against time: despair, false optimism, withdrawal.

The Significance of Time: Religion vs. Psychology

The psychotherapist and the counseling minister know better than anyone how maladjusted people find it difficult to come to grips with time. Both religion and psychology have in the past brought different emphases to bear upon the significance of time in human experience. Psychology has viewed most spiritual systems suspiciously because of their emphasis on happiness as a commodity of the future not easily available in this "vale of tears" we call life. Religion on the other hand has always been wary of any purely secularist attitude. It is absolutely essential then that the modern man be somehow given new insights which draw from both religion and psychology.

The accusation made against Christianity (or "religion" in general) of emphasizing an "optimism of withdrawal," as Teilhard calls it, is, from a psychotheological point of view, not without some justification. But our approach suggests that withdrawal is not necessarily the essence of religious experience. A mature religious outlook is broader than any body of doctrine. Man's yearning for happiness is as real as his appetite for food, yet as spiritual as his desire for love. Consequently, the only significant attitude is one which finds psychological justification as well as moral fulfillment.

True, we should never be willing to settle for the reassurances we receive in the here and now. Yet there are those who always seek eternal insurance policies against what is yet to happen; this is a perversion of hope and merely another way of clinging to the present. Christ often warned man against this tendency. "Can any of you, for all his worrying, add one single cubit to his span of life?" (Matthew 6, 27). He did not merely appeal to us to control our anxieties by recourse to providence. In a psychotheological context he points up how obsessive-compulsive gestures always make it difficult for us to submit to the subtle demands that any true resolution of anxiety makes in terms of the future. Conflicts are resolved for the purpose of reorienting a man's life; deepening one's awareness of the present is always a stepping-stone, a preparation for future maturity.

Thus, in a psychotheological sense the belief that the present is the focus of all experience is immoral. Sin is not merely a "turning of one's back on God"; it is a repudiation of any kind of resurrection, of the possibility of future engagement with life. It is immoral precisely because it limits a person's vision to the present moment. Extreme humanists see moral purposefulness as a pipe dream because they refuse to accept the reality of transcendence; but religion is just as narrow whenever it refuses to accept the fact that man's present moral struggle must be seen in an ever-changing evolutionary context.

There is a real challenge to the moral community in the fact that genuine involvement in the future is more often characteristic of the so-called humanist mentality. It is ironic that this should be so, as if the Christian continues to use vocabulary in which he no longer believes. The use of the traditional Christian concepts of hope and resurrection in a secular context (if indeed any human experience can ever be called purely secular) has caused a crisis in modern religion which goes to the very heart of its future relevance for the world, and the crisis will diminish only to the extent that psychological and moral drives are seen as one. Here, especially, the psychotheological approach would seem to be helpful. The dilemma of the believer who is caught between those who stress transcendent religious values and those who see nothing beyond human values becomes less of a problem only when one views moral and psychological approaches as synchronous.

If it is true that religious naiveté, however inadvertently, has prompted man to shrink back and become preoccupied with hopes of heaven, it is just as true that it has helped him cling to a sense of transcendence. Religious idealism will continue to be an important influence as long as it serves to remind us that the desire for happiness reflects a belief that man has every right to search for constant renewal, that man does not merely survive, but grows.

Religion has never been more on the defensive than it is today. We tend to take this fact for granted, but psychotheology is not reconciled to it. True religion can always help us see that man's desire for everlasting happiness has a basis in experience. Even so formalized a ritual as the Catholic confessional can provide a valid experience if understood and used correctly. But insofar as it tempts a man to retreat into introspection and self-centered morality, it is next to worthless.

The Abuse of the Past

Religion, more than psychology, continues to say a great deal about the "value of the past," in spite of the fact that for many persons today tradition is nothing more than deadwood. Those who continue to use history and tradition as their strongest weapon often do so merely as a propaganda device and turn regard for tradition into idolatry. There is nothing sacred about history except for what it can teach us. Psychotheology says that traditional religious customs and theological systems have real value only to the extent that they exercise psychological influence in the here-and-now.

An approach such as that of historian Frances Yates has a great deal to tell us in this regard and serves well in bringing religion and psychology closer together. She writes of the "memory theatre" — the process by which the past is seen in light of present experience. The American child, for example, who is asked to imagine George Washington and his troops gripped by the cold and suffering of Valley Forge is doing more than recalling an inspiring "fact of history." He is at the same time extending his vision in order to deepen a sensitivity not yet dynamically focused. Appreciation of the present moment, in other words, is enhanced by a new sensitivity about what has already happened. The present moment becomes even more intelligible in light of the past.

The application to religious history is obvious. Christian tradition can be made meaningful only to the extent that it makes present experience meaningful. Religion has seen the psychological value of the principle in its ritual, for example. But it has not gone far enough in its understanding of it. Christian history itself can be subjected to a process of sorting out valid and invalid moments. Those facts which record religious discord and moral blindness are not seen merely as "facts" but openly as what they are — aberrations. Likewise, valid moments stand ready to be relived, not merely recalled. The supreme test of any fact of Christianity's history is whether or not it can shed any light on the here-and-now. If it does not, it bears little relationship to whatever Christ, or any religious figure for that matter, tells us about man's struggle for happiness. Some may regard this attitude as too pragmatic and continue to insist that certain facts and events contain a value whether or not we see them as vital; psychotheology would insist that the recollection of the past either provides insight into the present or it does not.

It is foolish to be indifferent to history, but it is always immoral to use it to one's own ends. Religion has often seemed to use history to confirm its own prejudices — for example, man's proclivity to evil. But this uses the past as a psychologically perverse weapon to freeze man in a sense of hopelessness, to force him to hear nothing but the dreary echoes of how evil he is. The cynical can never use the past to any good end. Emerson spoke of this temptation:

"Our young people are diseased," he said, speaking of those who seemed to be conspiring against the future of the America of his time, "with the theological problems of original sin, origin of evil, pre-destination, and the like. These never presented a practical difficulty to any man, never darkened any man's road, who did not go out of his way to seek them." A basic psychospiritual law is to learn to use history for moral betterment, not merely as a reminder of mistakes.

Yet moral evils which have continued to plague man since time immemorial cannot be cavalierly dismissed; past aberrations serve to remind us constantly of the evil in men's hearts. Still, emotional and religious progress have never benefited from emphasizing the evils of the past in order to nurture anxiety. When a sense of failure becomes an exclusive psychological weapon, it cannot result in moral health. Psychotheologically then, history can serve only one function — to make the present alive.

We have much to learn from modern psychotherapeutic practice, and its insistence that preoccupation with past mistakes (even those which are firmly embedded in the memory and point up the "inevitability" of failure) affords little practical help to a person who is trying to make morality workable in the present. Anyone who has faith in moral ideals accepts the reality of moral evil, but only as a stepping-stone to the future.

Modern man is not bound by the concepts of a medieval psychology of sin and evil. Psychotheology sees both the virtue of hope and man's desire for happiness in terms of what the present portends for the moral future of mankind. The present must always be taken as the potential for future development. A man of limited vision, on the other hand, contracts his view until it makes for more despair than he can stand.

Today, desire for social perfection is part of the legacy of the 20th century. Through psychology, man has come to believe in the open-endedness, the continuing enlargement of his intellectual and emotional life, and this in spite of the past. As with the mystic of old, the religious quality of many modern experiences stems from a sense of pilgrimage; but it is essentially different because it is postulated upon a principle that man is psychologically open-ended. The introverted tendencies of the medieval moralist who spoke of combatting "self-will" and of "self-hatred" strike us as limited today, even though they reflected his search for a meaningful life. But his premise was that human nature was fixed and predictable. The moral courage of modern man consists precisely in the fact that his search has all the agony but few of the protections of the old attitude.

The modern notion of hope, psychotheologically speaking, emphasizes a wholistic appreciation of experience, one which sees even the irrational elements of human behavior as part and parcel of the redemption of our future society. Thus psychological insight and religious aspiration make of hope a single coin.

A Psychotheology of Hope

The future glory of which Christianity speaks may be seen as heaven by some persons, but it also contains a valid psychodynamic principle. The branch of psychology called psychoanalysis confirms this in its own way when it says that the unconscious wields more power in human motivation than we may be at first inclined to see. For a man to be fully functioning, it is necessary to introduce the power of the unconscious *id* to the conscious *ego*. In religious as well as psychological terms, no fact is ever fully understood except in light of what it can become and what future influence it will wield.

Psychotheology sees God himself as the future. To speak of God in this way is to translate the traditional dogma of God's eternity into psychological terms, to see him not merely as timeless but as the dynamic element in experience which keeps man's hope and sense of wonder alive. Whether this is reflected in intellectual speculation, as in mathematical projection, or in such theological terms as eschatology, it points up the fact that the future is constantly being enjoined and plundered by the unconsciousness of man which clings *for its very life* to its hope and aspiration. God does not merely give us something to hope for; he is the energy we call hope.

A true gospel of hope has its own definition of faith. Faith is based on the belief that life is a series of points in a journey toward the future. A man achieves workable perspectives of the present only as he proceeds from one point of unfolding convergence to the next. With what we have come to know of the workings of the human mind through psychology, we can even say that it is only through his trust in the future that a man can give coherence to present experiences.

In order to distill the full worth of what is still hidden in man's personal or collective future, we must see present experience phenomenologically linked to the future and not just abstractly joined to it. The challenge is to discover whether such a connection is based on more than vague aspiration, and to what extent.

Psychologists give substantiality to the power of hope when they speak of "forward memory," the power which shapes a man to the task of the present moment. Without it a person would not drive an automobile or even think of tomorrow. The extent to which this attitude becomes part of a man's moral life will give psychological depth to his moral actions. Whenever religion acknowledges the power of hope in this sense, it gives morality a deeper meaning and purpose. For example, in the season before Christmas known as Advent, Christians are told to prepare for the "coming of Christ." Psychotheologically speaking, they are doing more than preparing for the commemoration of an historical event; they are deepening an awareness, sharpening the power of anticipated vision, assuaging the anxiety that is born of their natural fear that what they as Christians look for has no reality. Thus, when renewed perceptions help the personality to face present experience, the future becomes less a source of terror. This is no less true of Christian mystery than of ordinary human experience.

In the past 300 years, man's definition of the future has changed radically. He has come to see that his future is intimately linked to and conditioned by the present. Religion in the traditional sense has lost its exclusive claim to the stewardship of man's hopes. This has caused a crisis in Western religious sensibility which perhaps even yet has to be acknowledged by religion itself. Psychotheology seeks to show that psychology can give traditional religious concepts about future salvation a new depth.

Mankind's hopes can always be seen in terms of either an after-life in heaven or a utopia on earth. The question, we suggest, is a semantic one. What is important is that any definition of salvation — heavenly or secular — has to be preceded by the psychodynamic principle that there is no future salvation without the reconciliation of men in the here-and-now. Christ alluded to this when he said that a person bringing a gift to the altar should first remember the brother he has offended, and be reconciled to him. This has never been acknowledged for the psychodynamic commandment it is.

We have always known that universal brotherhood is impossible without peace and unity; but it is only today that we realize more than ever that such a goal, however remote, is impossible without the opening of our hearts to one another. It is no longer a matter of pious aspiration; hope is a psychological necessity. When a person opens himself to others now, when he loves, he does so because he has full psychological realization that he is building for the future. That is probably why the forces of prejudice and racism, the anti-Christs of our time, are howling so loudly.

The presence of discord in the world continues to remind us of man's lack of faith in the future. This should not surprise us. The search for the future will always remain difficult as long as men reject dynamic religious values out of psychological blindness. In one of the starkest passages of the New Testament, Christ reminds us of the inevitability of our failures: "When an unclean spirit goes out of a man, it wanders through waterless country looking for a place to rest, and not finding one it says, 'I will go back to the home I came from.' But on arrival, finding it swept and tidied, it then goes off and brings seven other spirits more wicked than itself, and they go in and set up house there, so that the man ends up by being worse than he was before" (Luke 11, 24-26).

Many persons today continue to imagine that the discord characterizing our time results from the rejection of traditional Christian concepts of morality. We have even begun to speak (some of us with relish) of the "post-Christian" age. Psychotheologically this attitude carries little weight. Christianity is not so much dead as it is outgrowing its traditional and organizational character, assuming a new shape for the future. Incarnational values, as we have seen, expand as long as human consciousness expands. They grow and deepen with each century. The God who will take flesh among us in the future will not be the God of the past.

The God of the past was a God of authority. Men looked to him to bring order out of chaos — the essential condition being that all men submit to that authority, especially as manifested in this or that institution. But medieval notions of authority, be they invested in Church, government or family, are undergoing drastic changes. In a democratic society the image of God as some sort of king has never made any sense. An approach such as that of psychotheology, which insists on taking the facts of change and evolution into consideration, must show to what extent Christian moral principles are based upon psychological insights that do not depend upon outworn concepts, no matter how hallowed by the past. The God of the 21st century will speak in terms of human aspirations, will confirm man's instinctual love for the future. In psychotheological terms he will be a God who urges men to fulfill their highest potentialities, especially by means of psychic bonds which unite them in a common destiny. Christ himself always spoke of God in terms of a more abundant future for man. Christians who have faith cannot doubt for a moment that his futuristic vision must be theirs.

Still, for many people, Christ's claim to fame rests on the authority due to him because of his divine and miraculous power. Psychotheology limits discussion to a phenomenological area. Past debates over Christ's "nature" succeeded only in keeping Christ's real significance out of man's psychic grasp.

Certainly an insistence upon Christ's divinity never succeeded of itself in achieving the good for which he yearned and even gave up his life — the future of mankind. This was based on his acknowledgment that the hopes of those he cured were worthy of recognition. That the manifestations of Christ's concern for his fellow men took many therapeutic forms — the restoring of sight, the cleansing of leprosy, the forgiveness of sin, the restoration of psychological peace — is not nearly as important as the fact that they were moments in his *single vision,* his recognition of the reality of man's aspirations. Man's aspirations are always settings for the miracles; the supreme miracle is to help men to see as Christ did that their aspirations are not fantasies.

Man's quest for unity and happiness makes no sense apart from belief in the future — that his life can be changed, reordered, and reoriented. Moral blindness always stands ready to be enlightened by the man who allows himself to become more psychologically alive through hope. This premise alone would have guaranteed the survival of Christ's moral philosophy. Within the frame of values based on an all-forgiving God, forgiveness is the way we bless the future and make provision for it. Christ's exhortation that we must forgive not seven times but seventy times seven is still the most important principle in the psychotheological understanding of the future salvation of mankind. A morally cynical person will always be confounded by this Christian attitude; but no one can deny the dynamic implications of any act of real forgiveness.

Christ's attitude still differs in most respects from our own, and his vision led him to see beyond the selfishness of nations, races, and theological systems. If his ideal is still beyond our grasp, it is only because our religious and political institutions continue to be psychologically limited by the illusion of collective national or racial superiority. Christ's contemporaries likewise were afflicted by cultural blindness. But Christ's attitude was and still is futuristic and free.

Generosity continues to be difficult because it is predicated upon the narrow limits we ourselves impose. Conflicts between nations and religions are self-engendered conspiracies against the future. No institution which claims to be Christian can ignore the fundamental reality of mankind's hope to be unified. It is difficult only for those who have put love for Church or country before love for mankind's future.

What institutional moralists and pious politicians fail to see is that man's hope for salvation has to precede faith in any particular institution. Men want love and unity even before patriotism. They seek it out on every level of experience. Religion and psychology and politics all dictate to man about his life — his art, his sex life, his politics. But none of them, nor all of them in concert, can tell man what he already knows — that his future is in his own hands. Man knows limitations and anxieties which can become sources of new and future psychodynamic insights and which can also make him miserable. While religion and psychology both have brought their influence to bear upon important levels of human activity, no one has the exclusive means for helping man relate to the future through these experiences. Some underlying law of honesty requires man to locate his centers of conflict and to see for himself how such conflicts can be overcome — in short, how he can make his own personal experience self-revelatory. Even the help we receive from religion and psychology to love more deeply means before anything else that a man must learn to relate to life, in his own way.

In modern times psychology has stressed this fact by saying that anxieties disappear as a man realizes his powers to become "authentic." Religion, too, maintains that personal morality gives man a deeper sense of meaningful existence, a sense of purpose. But whether motivated by psychological or religious insight, authenticity can develop only out of a man's personal belief in his dedication to posterity. It does not matter that some men's sense of purpose is limited or practically non-existent. Man is always open to new forces in his life and in the lives of others, and it is this openness and purpose that religion and psychology must encourage.

When men allow themselves to be dominated, they lose their sense of hope. The need for reassurance is so strong for some people that they often take refuge in religious or psychological ritual. This leads to nothing more than continuing frustration. Any influence which keeps a man from understanding vital issues by confining him to this or that device deprives him of his right to fulfillment, even hampering his ability to relate to others. It impedes his sense of universal moral values. Christ's universal vision, on the other hand, knows no prejudice because it uses no protective devices except the goodness of the human heart.

In primitive religious experience the *shaman* or witch doctor created a climate of irresistible psychological conditions that resulted in emotional and even physical paralysis. This situation is

not outside the ken of our experience, for all our so-called sophistication. We know only too well how men allow themselves to be
hypnotized by religious and political propaganda. Blindness can
always be inflicted upon the ignorant in the name of authority.
Christ was well aware of the evil of such charlatanry and warned
of its inevitable disaster: "Can one blind man guide another?
Surely both will fall into a pit" (Luke 6, 39).

One of the most famous examples of Christ's honesty in this
regard is found in the New Testament episode of the woman
caught in adultery. Her accusers demanded death by stoning as
required by the law of Moses. From a psychodynamic point of
view, Christ's refusal to condemn her was more than an exercise
in compassion; his tenderness was at the same time a condemnation of her accusers. They refused to acknowledge the uniqueness
of her personality or her right to readjust her life. The stones they
were about to hurl were symbols of their own psychic blindness, of
a morality that had become rigid. Christ knew that even the most
pathetic human weaknesses reflect hopes that need to be recognized
and understood, to be given room to change for future experience.
He knew the right to hope precedes whatever immoral shape our
experience may take. The sin of the woman's accusers was even
more reprehensible than her adultery, for in their arrogance they
sought to isolate her from others, to freeze her to the present moment of despair.

Christ warns anyone who assumes the role of judge — be he a
moralist, a psychologist or a politician — that the judge runs the
risk of committing the only real sin: denying the birthright of
every human being to hope. People who have conflict in their lives,
who are overwhelmed by a sense of failure and even despair, need
not be reminded of their inadequacies, their lack of skills, the
tasks they have bungled. Even in their sense of frustration, they
must be kept open to the possibility of change. Too often their
sense of being at odds with themselves and others is compounded
by a society which has lost its own sense of hope and renewal.

This has been obvious in the past when moralists attempted to
classify behavior as either virtuous or sinful, neglecting the sub-
jective needs of each individual. For many persons even today,

contrition continues to be ritual whereby the "sinner" seeks to "buy back" God's favor. Psychology has brought a new depth to such a narrow interpretation of human motivation. Yet today even psychological counseling stands in danger of committing what religion has perpetrated in the past. The psychologist who concentrates on mechanistic explanations for anxiety, who merely enumerates the psychic factors underlying conflictual behavior, puts his desire to fit personalities into his own pre-conceived categories before their need. All men have been babies, he says; all have had parents, all have known the classic psychic struggles. Classifying human behavior becomes more important than the personal drive for meaningful change.

An authoritarian institution which inhibits self-understanding is, in terms of the future, severely limited. A man who has not located the sources of hope within *himself* will always move through life with a lingering sense of dissociation, his power to make judgments clouded, his belief in the redemptive power of experience ineffective. Such a man will never acquire a sense of genuine moral responsibility. In psychotheological terms this is true immorality, for one's moral sense has been psychically inhibited.

Nowhere is it more imperative that religion and psychology illuminate each other than in regard to the future. In their common desire to help man overcome his conflicts, religion and psychology must use whatever traditional stratagems they can jointly call into play. They must, before all else, take cognizance of the importance of man's sense of aspiration.

For example, repentance in religion is traditionally coupled with self-effacement before God and man. But this kind of humility is a psychic phenomenon as well as a virtue, and therefore humility must express itself before anything else as an energy which keeps man open to the future, open to new ways of experiencing. The traditional religious emphasis on self-contempt has little meaning in a world which thinks in cosmic terms.

In the same way, many energies which are thought to concern man's psychic life exclusively must be brought to play an important role in his religious life. Imagination is a generative force, morally as well as psychologically. Man's poetic fantasies have often been dismissed by moralists as untrustworthy and even as a source of potential immorality. Still, men must be allowed free reign for their fantasies and their hopes. In psychological terms, we all have the right to "as if" situations. The crippled people who came to Christ were in that sense already cured. Christ dealt with their aspirations most sympathetically. After listening to them, Christ often said, "Your faith deserves it, so let this be done for you." He saw that even fantasy can be put to the service of reality. The true healer is one who stands ready to help a man align his aspirations with what can become reality.

In the psychoanalytic technique known as "free association," we see an important use of the virtue of hope. Freud discovered and developed this process as a profound means of investigating the unconscious. Out of a random sampling of thoughts, sensations and feelings, he saw the possibility of a psychic convergence which could result in the possibility of future health.

In light of this principle, religion can come to appreciate more fully what role that hope can play for a man, even in terms of the man's moral weaknesses. Even the power that theologians refer to as "grace" is, in a psychotheological context, an appreciation of how the promise of the future can transform people. In whatever sense grace is a mystery, it is also a future hope, for it is mostly an unconscious factor of religious experience that becomes increasingly operational as one grows in the awareness of becoming morally alive. Grace has become accessible by believing that even what seems apparently worthless and perhaps immoral does indeed have a worth beyond itself.

Hope, in psychotheological terms, is a power whose stirrings continue to remind us that man must always look to experiences which have yet to become realities. What may seem like wishful thinking, make-believe, or even frustration, may be the first step in a breakthrough to a new life.

Through hope we keep ourselves open to whatever epiphany experience is ready to unveil. We learn to worship God whose relationship to the world remains constantly alive and constantly revealing. That is why to be illuminated and strengthened by hope is, in terms of the future, our only authentic prayer.

7

AUTHORITY

The inability to understand and exercise authority has been one of the most serious problems of our age. The nature of the problem, impinging on every level of human experience, has received comment from both religion and psychology. Some religious leaders have emphasized blind submission, while psychologists have held more permissive attitudes. But as long as authority is viewed as an outer force that intrudes upon one's inner world, it will always remain a stumbling block.

Self-Authority

A psychotheological approach has discovered a clearer understanding of the problem of authority in Christ's life. In Christ we see the fundamental issue of dominance and submission clearly mirrored. For a Christian, Christ is the ground where supreme power and love meet receptive, passive humanity. Any true answer to the question of authority must lie somewhere in his life.

True independence and self-realization are attained only when a man sees himself as author of his own autobiography. Each man writes his own life history insofar as life is fully experienced and as a person becomes free of the childish dependence of immaturity. A man grows as he learns to perfect his own power for insights and revelations. Thus, when we speak of God's authority in psychotheological terms, we mean not merely an external, fear-inducing command, but a compelling power which calls forth the deepest expressions of the human personality. The need to depend upon God as an authority may be necessary when a person is really helpless and has no one to turn to in his distress. But this reliance should give way to a true regard for one's personality, bringing with it new hope and morale. This renewal, more than anything else, opens up new channels of maturity. The shift to a less dependent condition develops as an individual comes to believe that renewal is possible.

The mature independence demanded by God points to the future. It promises to make real each man's desire to be mature. However, it is the individual himself who achieves the goal, and a person leads the way for his own future only by participating in experience. This historical requirement leads him to look closely at how authority and maturity are related. First, it brings him to a fuller understanding of how he is both limited and enlarged by his psychic heritage, for he is the sum total of those forces which he inherits. The sense of authority which flows from his psychic heritage is awesome because it compels him to seek his own fulfillment. The Christ of the New Covenant was himself the culmination of such a search.

Authority, therefore, is the ability to draw from one's experience in such a way that personal vision has an organic relationship to the entire community. In this sense, only the man who is independent is in a position to be more understanding to his fellow man. And it is only in this sense that authority as a force has any relevance to the destiny of mankind.

The Christian, like Christ, has moral authority. He is the continuing expression of Christ, and, before that, of Abraham and Moses. Unconsciously, he represents Buddha-nature and Rama-Krishna as much as he does Cardinal Newman and John Wesley. But he also stands in witness of the Inquisition and the "holy" wars. His mythic dimension, like that of the Hindu, must be to locate within himself those valid sources of moral authority which go to make his meaning.

Unfortunately there are many pitfalls in the search for personal authority. It is easy to bargain for "certainty" at the expense of adventure and progress. The individual who concludes that the narrow boundaries of his own culture or community must apply to a universal value system falls prey to his own delusions of grandeur. This type of bias is, in the psychotheological sense, a kind of idolatry, for when a person settles for a parochial vision of life, he may find himself worshiping the opinions and acquisitions of his culture alone. If sin is a departure from that which is most universally fulfilling, then this type of idolatry becomes a pathetic kind of sinfulness. God, as reported by Ezekiel, rebuffs this attitude: "Son of man, these people have enshrined their own idols in their hearts, they cling to the cause of their sins; am I going to be consulted by them?" (Ezekiel 14, 2-3).

When man assumes moral authority, he participates in a creative act. He can only participate, or be "consulted," as he continues to mature. This means going beyond the narrow codes of his particular culture. It means being able to opt for a universal morality which in a Christian sense is benevolence and peacemaking. People who search for genuine independence stand on the side of what the future demands; they nearly always find themselves at odds with their own environment. They may even be forced into disobedience when faced with immoral leadership. Their sense of right causes them to question sentiments like "my country, right or wrong" and to take up the cause of being radically independent, rather than acting as mere pawns of a particular authoritarian structure, be it government or Church.

Psychoanalysis has helped us to see the meaning of authority figures by placing great emphasis upon the role of transference. Each person may, at times, see an authority as the likeness of early significant figures in his own life. This is particularly helpful in therapy where a reworking of conflict requires the presence of a "transference neurosis." What the psychoanalyst may fail to see is that most transference is also personal striving, for it works to introduce the individual to areas of his own self which he both fears and strives to attain. Thus a constant cycle of renewal is based in part on an individual's search for a sense of independence and meaning within his personal and cultural history. Each person is the product of an historical progression, yet somehow free of it. His dilemma is how he is to accept some of his background while rejecting other parts. The man who is "a chip off the old block" may have found more of whom he wishes to be in his father than in his mother. He then becomes something like the father, even to the point of having similar facial expressions and using speech mannerisms which reflect the subtleties of personality his father introduced. But as he strives to be free, even the "chip off the old block" may ultimately have serious reservations about identifying with his father. Every man wishes to make it on his own, to write his own autobiography as well as contribute to the "uncreated conscience of his race."

To accept progress is, in a psychotheological sense, to grow both in mental health and virtue. It allows for a sense of openness. But openness can never be arrived at until a person comes to terms with just what his independence means. An individual must be willing to explore all of his transferential responses, whether they are based upon unconscious identification with a parent or with the "security" of the past. Jesus said to his disciples in a similar vein: "Be on guard against the yeast of the Pharisees — that is, their hypocrisy" (Luke 12, 1). This did not detract from the dedication of the Pharisees (who were, after all, the religious authorities), but it did warn against the temptation to follow their prejudices. Likewise, since each person's obligation to his own age and to his work for the future remains paramount, he finds himself with the necessity of rooting out areas of parental transference. Certain emotional disturbances arise from the fact that a person may fear he is becoming too much like his parent. This leads to a kind of caricature; his identity becomes blurred, since it tosses aside any real notion of what personality really is. A man who is afraid of stepping into his father's shoes reacts strongly to distinguishing between himself and an effigy of his parent. A man who fears he is too much like his father may easily fall into the trap of reacting violently against some of his own essence and instead become a restless seeker. The so-called "phony" in Western culture is often an individual inventing "better parents" who can never exist for him, rather than looking to all of the enrichments with which his own personality can provide him.

The basis for selfhood cannot rest ultimately in a man's experiences with authority. Every Christian is in the process of *becoming* more like Christ, not merely caricaturing him. His psychic frontiers must constantly be expanding so that he reaches a stance of universal and, ultimately, cosmic concern, as Christ did. This is the sense of maturity of the *new man* who keeps faith with the triumph of Christ's mission as the universal leveler. A new sense of authority is born. "But as we have the same spirit of faith that is mentioned in Scripture — *I believed, and therefore I spoke* — we too believe and therefore we too speak, in our turn, and put us by his side and you with us" (2 Corinthians 4, 13-14). The stake people then share would be more like Christ and would raise the individual beyond the confines of even his own background, even beyond the title "Christian."

The analytic psychology of Carl Jung has recognized that the problem of becoming an individual must go beyond the fear of being like one's parents. A person must seek himself through the collective unconsciousness with which life provides him. In the same way, the Christian must go beneath and beyond mere identification with or rebellion against the established Church. Instead, he must seek to individuate his life so that he recognizes that he exists under the influence of the Holy Spirit, an influence which permeates every aspect of his life but which can never rob him of his independence. This individuation is, in psychotheological terminology, the authenticity of personal experience as a universal ethic. The venture of becoming a person means becoming more of a participant in the evolutional process of creation.

The search for God begins only when one is willing to release his claim to established identities, even what he thinks to be Christ's. He must recognize that he is involved in history and must therefore not clutch at the easiest version of God. His true authority as a Christian comes to him only as he departs even from society's predetermined notion of who Christ is.

Christ's great contemporary, John the Baptist, understood this. He disavowed any personal claim to being the Messiah. His identity was his own, as a seeker in his own right. It might have been tempting for him to interpret his vast following as an indication that he could play the role of Christ. He was content, however, to be who he was, "a witness." His autobiography was to be his own. When it was time to give him a name, his mother insisted that his name be John rather than Zechariah. He was, in fact, named after no one of his own immediate lineage and was to be unencumbered by the transference problems which frequently accompany a son.

Needless to say, John became an exemplification of the movement *toward* Christ. He was content to help move history in the direction of a fuller humanization of the religious values of the Old Testament. Each attempt a person makes to seek a "new world" is a necessary prelude to the time when narrowness and sin will be followed by universal communication and fulfillment. This is no static concept foretelling the arrival of a celestial playland. Rather, it is the sacramental view of how man, more than all other creatures, seeks a future which is more profound and loving. This is always the result when men — acting as the creatures of the world, and therefore as the sons of the Creator — strive to build a better earth. John the Baptist exemplified this creative enterprise. Unlike the mythic Sisyphus who was condemned forever to pushing a boulder up a mountain only to see it roll to the other side, John the Baptist began from where he was and accomplished what he set out to do. He had no pretensions. He was his own authority. He knew he could not reduce the office of Christ to himself. He did not pretend, as Sisyphus did, to be the sole end of creation. He used his own means, the baptism of water, but he foresaw himself without arrogance as preparing for a better future.

That is why John still exemplifies the archetypal model of authentic independence. Christ called John more than a prophet in that his claim was based on his own experience. John wanted to know who he himself was, he was more interested in this than in setting out warnings. He was a participant-observer in the birth of Christianity. His personal participation made for his self-awareness. The person who so knows himself is always the actual authority. Thus, in submitting to John's baptism, Christ suggested that John's role, like that of a true authority figure, was not to dominate but to shed light and to enlarge.

Authority and Brotherhood

The submission of Christ to John on the banks of the Jordan is one of the most striking incidents in Christ's life because it tells us that he and John met not as student and teacher, or as son and father, but as brothers, sharing in an act that enriched both of them. John emerges in this context as a herald, a sentinel of brotherhood and unification. John's earlier role was explicitly one of preparation. In this regard he could clearly be seen as authority, since his immediate rendezvous was with the historical imperative of trusting the future. When he baptized Jesus, he resembled Joseph, the son of Jacob. Joseph, like John, was a servant of the future. His brothers were at first required to submit to him, but in a little while he revealed his mission to them: "Come closer to me. . . . I am your brother Joseph whom you sold into Egypt. But now, do not grieve, do not reproach yourselves for having sold me here, since God sent me before you to preserve your lives" (Genesis 45, 4-5). In this beautiful statement Joseph made clear that although he was first in authority because of his position, he now wished to serve his brothers and to share in their lives, in their sorrows and their joys.

John the Baptist removed himself from the position of being the promised Messiah. He was able to use his sense of authenticity in ways which would not have him acting falsely in order to gain reputation and glory. Instead of being neurotic self-abnegation, his humility was the exercise of virile authority. Although, he declared, referring to the Christ who was to follow, "I am not fit to undo his sandal strap," he did make clear what his own role was: "I have seen and I am the witness that he is the Chosen One of God" (John 1, 27-34). The figure of speech John used was merely an expression. What was important for him was to be able to do what he felt was right and correct without distorting his task because of neurotic needs.

This often misunderstood incident, like that of John's confrontation with Jesus at the river, was an approach to a new understanding of the nature of authority. The keynote, of course, is that true authority *serves* as well as *commands*. John's dilemma remains the peril of the mid-20th century where the cry for "law and order" is sometimes a reenforcement of command rather than a real attempt to understand historic perspectives. Both Joseph and John were benevolent in that they made way for the future. Neither of them could be said to be a reactionary. Any true leader, whether he be teacher, prophet, government official, or parent, is one who seeks out the searching dynamic of love in his dealings with those who need guidance. This moral leadership seeks a point where it welcomes and trusts others, as Joseph welcomed his brothers and as John welcomed Christ.

Christ's meeting with John taught him a great deal. In turn he used the incident to show his followers that he agreed essentially with the definition of authority which John exemplified. John did not relinquish his authority when he baptized Jesus, any more than Jesus later relinquished his authority when he was crucified. Submission to a higher will is, in psychotheological terms, always a stepping-stone to communion, that point where the social order has learned to depend less upon manipulation. John did not live up to cultural expectations. He refused to be seen as the Christ, just as Jesus refused to be seen as the great military messiah who would violently deliver Israel from her enemies. The transferential expectation which their culture placed on them had to be confronted and denied in order for something more noble and loving to be born. Christ had to "resolve" this transference, this identity struggle, by attempting to convince the authorities of the Jewish community that his concept of authority was not the kind they had been famliar with.

From a psychotheological vantage point, the modern era is struggling to extend the concept of authority in keeping with the new revelations of psychiatry, offering new insights of man as a moral agent. The Pharisees of old were threatened by Christ's challenge to their concept of authority, since anyone who tried even temporarily to discard its traditional mantle was viewed as a threat to the social order. People today who are searching for a charismatic identity are as much a threat to the "establishment" as Christ was then. Suspicions always run wild when cultural stagnation is challenged. Christ sought to serve the poor, the have-nots, the hated tax collectors and in so doing he was re-working the whole notion of what a leader was expected to do. He touched off the sparks of a revolution which proclaimed a new equality among men and the fact that arrogant superiority and authentic authority would always be distinguishable.

The ecclesiastical and political authorities who destroyed him did so because they were threatened by his deemphasis of the external forms of authority, because he sought to enter into friendship with those whom they despised. But anything less could not have been possible for a man with his vision. We have the same experience and become like Christ when we discover how loving, open, free, and equal we feel in the presence of those who are free and independent.

The entry of a new member into any established organization always represents a threat to orthodox persons. When Christ began his public preaching, the collective concern of the Jewish community was stricken with foreboding and anguish. His first disciples were Jews who — unlike the religious leaders — were opening their religious beliefs to exploration. Paul at first rejected them. He testified after his conversion to the contempt in which he had held the new leveling doctrines. Paul, before his conversion, was a perfect example of the frenzy to which a traditionalist can be driven when he fears the loss of old values.

When he later welcomed Gentiles into the Christian community, Paul gave testimony to the fact that the old rationale of the ruling power had come to an end. The chosen people were not simply to live because of a heritage of blood. "I owe a duty to Greeks just as much as to barbarians, to the educated just as much as to the uneducated" (Romans 1, 14). Christ's word had become the great leveler. Mankind was now envisioned as expansive and communal. "Now in Christ Jesus, you that used to be so far apart from us have been brought very close, by the blood of Christ. For he is the peace between us" (Ephesians 2, 13-14). The organic tissue which creates the body of mankind became psychologically and spiritually alive, a full expression of peace between men. And it is this expression of leadership which Paul manifested in his ability to reach out to many people. His experience was one of convergent reconciliation: "God in Christ was reconciling the world to himself" (2 Corinthians 4, 19). The spiritual factor became one of unity. The true leader reconciled mankind, and out of this reconciliation is born God, the total symbol of moral authority.

Convergence for each person is a goal characterized by both peace and excitement. Fulfillment comes to each person as he confirms his interrelationship to the world around him. The goal of psychotherapy is to provide a modicum of happiness based upon participation with other persons in one's world. This amiability with life is one of the chief sources of creativity. From the standpoint of religion, man seeks his peace in God. However, the act of reconciliation with God must engage the individual in acts of mercy and love. The reality of personal commitment to the divine Creator is a constant conversion of motives and actions in the direction of true meaningfulness. St. Paul says, "We know that by turning everything to their good God cooperates with all those who love him, with all those that he has called according to his purpose" (Romans 8, 28).

Some people cling tenaciously to their narrow notions about authority. In a group dynamics situation, for example, it can frequently be observed how members of a small group who have rigid ideas about authority being similar to a "boss parent" will often jeer at anyone from their own ranks who manifests real leadership qualities. The rigid members find it easier to put up with the dominance of an unknown outside person than to accept the genuine leadership of one of their own. The prophet who finds no welcome in his own home is a concept as familiar to social scientists as it was to Christ. Authentic moral leadership can come about only when a group begins to see within its midst the beginnings of a real change in history.

Psychoanalysis points up the function of resistance in preserving the individual psyche. Resistances to moral change are experienced in similar ways. Further, the collective ego, like the individual ego, fears change. True authority never exists merely to preserve the *status quo*. It is rather the continuation of all gestures which in the past have made even the slightest impact upon how men are to relate to each other. Each person has within him something of the power to bring to life the Incarnation. This power will always be resisted as long as there are resistant forces at work in the world. All prophets are prepared for revolution as much as for revelation. One cannot take place without the other.

To reveal and to change — to prophesy and to change the world — are the marks of any true reformer. The ability to see hope in the hopeless and to recognize life in what had been thought to be death — these are the marks of authentic leadership and authority. "Out of the lame I will make a remnant, and out of the weary a mighty nation" (Micah 4, 7). This is the groundwork for the revolution inherent in the beatitudes where the "gentle . . . shall have the earth for their heritage" and "the peacemakers . . . shall be called the sons of God" (Matthew 5, 9). All prophecy and revolution are authority in process of becoming realized.

As men grow from self-protection to a kind of openness, it becomes possible to see the emergence of leadership as we have been trying to describe it. At one time in history it was essential to keep the monarch apart from his people. Obviously, it is easier to accept an august ruler than it is to become open to the challenge of the strange voice that, like John's, calls from the wilderness. John's mission foretold Christ's. In the case of Jesus, when he finally confronted his contemporaries with the destiny of God's will, they made light of his claim and, in a gesture of extreme irony, placed the crown of thorns upon his head.

Prophets and revolutionaries are always the harbingers of new insight and revelations. Psychotherapists know only too well how new disclosures in the process of therapy can cause resistance on the part of the patient. Likewise, whole communities may react negatively to any person or force that threatens their *status quo*. Christ's crucifixion, John the Baptist's beheading, Paul's imprisonment and trials — all demonstrate the resistance that challenges any voice of social change.

Christian sensibility is a prime way of realizing the leadership and authority of everything that makes man more conscious of his sacredness. This sense of moral leadership based upon reconciliation is the prophetic expression of the human community. It rises above temporary or arbitrary opinions which fail to welcome the future, whether these opinions are given by a pope, a president, or a potentate. Every man is his own infallible authority when he seeks to become a more honest expression of his potential. Thus what was "true" for one generation may not be true for the next. This is not because truth is unreliable, but because it adapts dynamically to the conditions of man as he faces experience. Traditional concepts of tribalization of the family and economic structure must constantly give way to future demands. Infallibility is no mere legal fiction, for the authority of the community of God is consistent with man's growth and development.

Psychotheology equates new psychological insights with the expression of human morality. The ego, in addition to being the synthesizing member of the human psyche, is also the foundation of moral unity. Every community has its own ego — that moral force which insures mankind's evolution; but obviously the only authority which is in any way capable of unifying the human race is love. St. John said: "No one has ever seen God; but as long as we love one another God will live in us and his love will be complete in us" (1 John 4, 12). The authority of John the Baptist, like that of any prophet, was one of great love and expectation, and the proclamation of this love is the only real expression of moral leadership.

Love must be expressed. It does no good to speak of it in abstract terms. A man's love for his wife, a parent's love for a child, a pastor's loving concern for his flock — these are the real areas of fulfillment. The impasses which keep a man from truly loving concern both psychotherapy and religion. In the former case, the lack of trust which had roots dating from infantile deprivation is seen as a root cause of alienation. Of course, there are no single causes. Cultural deprivation and constitutional endowments are other causal factors. But it will not be long before the social and medical sciences learn how to remedy these inequities. We are coming to understand what religion means when it says that love is manifested in grace and that man is the heir to love. It is man's heritage to recognize the primacy of love: "We can be sure that we love God's children if we love God himself and do what he has commanded us" (1 John 5, 2). Love therefore always leads to self-fulfillment, to self-actualization. Men seek love despite their possible fear of it. Psychology and religion must work to assist people in the true task of loving. But no man can love unless he loves himself. Love in this sense is self-knowledge, and the task remains to know oneself as the prelude to love.

The imaginative psychotherapist knows that his authority comes from his ability to introduce a person to himself. This promulgation of self-knowledge can take place only when the therapist respects his patient's moral right to independence. The patient becomes the prototype of Christ and the therapist a prototype of John the Baptist. For the healer, the person in need is always the one who is served. This, as psychotheology views it, is the only real expression of divine grace in our time. Due homage must be given to the individual psyche in the search for fulfillment. In many ways this homage corresponds to the sacrament of penance; the priest who has respect for the penitent's world is more truly a moral authority than the confessor who sees morality simply as a rigid system of "do's" and "dont's." Moreover, the degree of respect that a healer has for the other's world is the only way to measure how well he can minister to a person's needs. Love without participation is meaningless, since it fails to acknowledge the reality of the other person.

Thus the expert who assumes the mantle of authority aids another person only to the extent that he attempts to understand the progressively unfolding nature of the other. The most competent authority is the one who understands not only the outer terrain, but the inner as well. The inevitable question of situation ethics comes into account when personal values are discussed in relation to a larger evolving moral order. It is here that leadership as we have been discussing it becomes more comprehensible. The psalmist sings: "Yahweh is looking down from heaven at the sons of men, to see if a single one is wise, if a single one is seeking God" (Psalm 14, 2). The sense of community must be expressed individually. This does not mean that individual vision detracts from collective values. People who feel trust and love will invariably seek reconciliation in their own lives through a growing world sense. The leadership of a therapist or clergyman, parent or teacher, is most authentically expressed when it is based on the primary obligation of acknowledging another person's experience as authentic. This respect does not turn the authority figure into a mere "yes man." In fact, he needn't fear his critical abilities if he keeps faith with a person's right to seek self-determination.

In the therapy situation, the seeker's characteristic fear and his resistance to his own inner voice are the proper material for the therapist's elucidation: It is his task to point up relationships between the methods of dealing with strange situations so that the subject is better able to see how he is fleeing from his own inner, untapped spontaneity.

An example such as this certainly has value for other expert-seeker relationships which also demand the acknowledgment that strange forces are at work in all relationships. The counselor must admit, at least to himself, that his only possible motive in probing into the soul and mind of another person must be to bring the latter out of his sense of estrangement into a world of equality and community. The authority, as he becomes more a listener, learns to be on guard against the infantile wishes of the speaker if he wishes the relationship eventually to be equalized and the seeker to become mature.

Authority must be equalized. That is what the black man of today means when he says that he can no longer look to his white brother for "leadership." His vocation is to declare his independence in order to emphasize his eventual interdependence. Black separatists look to the day when they have redeemed their right to be fully "heard" on totally equal grounds with members of the white community. Like the Jews of old, God says to the blacks and to any oppressed people: "I carried you on eagles' wings and brought you to myself" (Exodus 19, 4). The people of God are fulfilled as they reach independence.

Like the early Israelites who were slaves in Egypt, black people in America will never rest in their subjugation. To do so would be to make an idol of the white power structure. The exercise of true authority rests in the process of growth and maturation. All people who keep faith with the future cannot fail to cast their lot with the blacks, the peacemakers, and "those who are persecuted in the cause of right" (Matthew 5, 10), since the future belongs to them. True authority casts out the idols of inequality. In this sense, history dictates the particular struggle of the time. *Each era demands the highest good.*

Although Moses rebuked his people for erecting an idol, he never lost faith in their ability to reach the land of Israel. He served as the eyes and ears of his people, trusting their increasing maturity. It was up to them to remain on the side of life and the future. He encouraged them: "Choose life then, so that you and your descendants may live in the love of Yahweh your God, obeying his voice, clinging to him; for in this your life consists" (Deuteronomy 30, 19-20). He blessed the tribes he had led across the desert. Obviously he knew that they would lose faith and then reclaim it. The essential message was his ability to bless and believe his people.

The psychotheological notion of authority demands that it acknowledge the other person's essential promise. This is basic for contemporary man who needs to receive blessings from a society which has kept faith with the future. A man who is willing to work for the greatest social good is our only saint, and a mature man is willing to assume the cloak of authority in order to work for the betterment of society. His outlook can afford to be radical since he can celebrate the excitement of renewal only as people have increased opportunities. He can see beyond the myth of race and national boundaries. He is not given to simplistic labels; "communism," "capitalism" and "anarchy" are not used by him for hasty condemnation. He sees the hope and aspiration in all human sentiments. Darwin, Marx, and Freud are not foreign to his world-view, and in fact they are incorporated into his personal steps into the future. He is willing to see the prophets and saints of tomorrow, whether they are labeled "new left," "black nationalist," or "progressive Christian." He can distinguish good faith from those forces which proclaim a lack of faith with the future.

Such a man, alive with moral authority, lifts himself to the heights for which he was created — being alive without constant reassurance or need for approval. Sharing in the divine life is always a creative enterprise for a Christian. His authority is therefore based on his striving for potentialities, although it may mean years of wandering before the actual breakthroughs. If there are persons who, like John the Baptist, are waiting for their own Christhood to be realized, then we can believe that people grow at their own pace. A man must be capable of recognizing his independence as it comes to fruition. The promise of the Messiah to the children of Israel symbolizes the expectation each man must ultimately have of himself and of his community. The appearance, when it happens, can be likened to the experience of giving birth. The prophet Isaiah sings: "As a woman with child nears her time and writhes and cries out in her pangs, so are we, Yahweh, in your presence: we have conceived, we writhe as if we were giving birth" (Isaiah 26, 17-18). The new offspring differs for each person; it is born of his longing for the messianic. Each new birth is steeped in mystery, for a person aspires to know the unknown depths of his own personality. The theme of modern psychoanalysis — that each person weds his inner richness with his outward consciousness — finds correspondence here. The spiritual claims of the Judeo-Christian tradition are represented by a godhead who stands for transformation and renewal. But men fall and give up their claim. The Egyptian and Babylonian gods were idols who bartered protection for personal offerings, and as long as a distorted notion of God's authority still influences mankind, the bartering still goes on. Deals are made with political forces in order to insure the *status quo*. The "establishment" demands homage in order to reward those who lack the courage to face a divinity without a specific name. The God of Abraham spoke through Moses and the prophets. The fulfillment of his all-pervasive sense of divinity is realized in transforming the world.

The mandate of Jesus must be lived in each age as styles and times dictate, and it becomes clarified as a particular social or psychological issue becomes centralized. The message of each age is eternally reflected in the mandate: "Not with you alone do I make this covenant today . . . but with him also who is not here today, as well as with him who stands with us here in the presence of Yahweh our God" (Deuteronomy 29, 13-15). Moses spoke of God's engagement with mankind, and the process is eternal, the stuff of history.

Even the authority of what Christianity calls the Holy Spirit can never be made so specific that it negates individual conscience. God's law proclaims the rightness of being alive and of being a productive force in the reconciliation of all mankind. Any formal theology may tend to compromise itself as it yields to the pressures of a frightened crowd. Even Aaron the priest yielded to panic and built a golden calf. People despair and sometimes demand pitiful reassurances from their leadership. When this happens, profanation takes place. Mankind is too dynamic for mere reassurance. Any reassurance has a high price tag for it always contradicts man's potentialities. Leadership which is aimed at reassurance misses opportunities for surprise and spontaneity. Psychotherapy or religion at its purest does not merely pacify. Rather, it helps a person to loosen himself from any dependence, even dependence on the outer trappings of an establishment. Only as this is accomplished does a person come to see that genuine authority does more than merely soothe.

The moral authority of a true value system never offers comfort *per se*. Instead, it challenges those who subscribe to it to engage in the revolutionary struggle of changing the world. Religion which emphasizes reassurance usually bases its claims on a god and a society which are static. God, on the other hand, is more than the past. He is courage and love. These are not mere attributes of a reassuring paternalism. Rather, they are operational principles which mankind either accepts on its journey or rejects. The course of the future will be marked by many chances and changes, but if the underlying concepts are humane and courageous, then progress will be made.

This new day of the Lord will manifest itself as people draw closer to the humanizing influences of freedom. There is a risk that many will shrink from liberation and continue to look for security in the repressiveness of powerful leaders and tribal gods.

Obviously the leadership which is truly needed goes beyond reassurance, since reassurance is bound to frustrate man's openness to the future. True authority is based on moral courage.

Authorities ought to make their presence less necessary. Parental authority, when properly exercised, assures the welfare of the child, but not to the point of depriving him of his freedom. The adult who is able to respond to the pulse of a situation rather than impose his own decrees follows in the steps of John. Christ declared: "You will learn the truth and the truth will make you free" (John 8, 32). Man seeks new covenants which will give him a foothold in the future. Christ's life is the bloodstream of the community. Christ is present even when he is not invoked by his traditional name.

Everything in the life of the historic Christ foretells his abiding presence. His miracles were human actions of healing and caring. But miracles become anachronistic if their influence ceases. No acts of love which Christ put into action have lost their vitality. They are still departure points of all forward movement in the search for human welfare. In his actions Christ was demonstrating a power beyond the acts themselves. The healing of one man is a symbol of all helping relationships. Each miracle was a leap ahead, and each person touched by Christ had to have a new view of life. The injunction to sin no more is, psychotheologically, the human duty to seek a position in life where people and things take on a deeper significance. In this context, a leader's command calls for a kind of transcendence where each man regains the value of his own life. A leader has the mission of being a guide and helpmate. Jesus was clear about this point when He stated: "You know that among the pagans the rulers lord it over them, and their great men make their authority felt. This is not to happen among you. Anyone who wants to be great among you must be your servant, and anyone who wants to be first among you must be your slave, just as the Son of Man came not to be served but to serve, and to give his life as a ransom for many" (Matthew 20, 26-28).

The concept of leadership which Christ believed in has revolutionized the definition of what authority ought to be — to serve, to be committed, to give one's life in love. The spectrum of what it means to command was transformed. Still, the effects of this revolution have yet to be felt on any major scale. Religious leaders have failed to see how the insights of psychoanalysis ratify Christ's teaching. The psychoanalyst, as a listener and a guide, allows himself to lead by providing corrective emotional experiences. The psychoanalytic influence in the fields of applied group dynamics and family counseling has provided a new type of leadership. The "teaching" task of the therapist, the group leader, and the family counselor is one of humbly waiting for the potential of an individual or a group to shine through the clouds of psychopathology. This new leader makes his moral choice by recognizing the blocks to maturity in his patient, penitent or group, and from there he encourages the emergence of adulthood. In line with this, he must recognize his own resistances to development. This sometimes involves renouncing his need for obeisance from his patient in order to encourage a more equal relationship.

The leaders of new revolutions will have to define their mission as one in which the basic dignity and equality of men are emphasized. The demands of the future are not revealed. However, from a Christian point of view, "all we know is that, when it is revealed, we shall be like him because we shall see him as he is" (1 John 3, 2). All mankind must share in the concept of authority which the future holds out, when men shall talk as Christ. The spirit of all true revolution is basic to divine revelation since God is the choice of life as opposed to death. He is progress as opposed to regression.

God is that common denominator which mankind achieves through moral and psychological growth. He is the equalizing force in the community of living beings. He makes humanity one, in one experience. The dwelling place of divinity is within the psychic unity of the human bond. David celebrated this theme in the words of a psalm: "Since all are my brothers and friends, I say 'Peace be with you!' Since Yahweh our God lives here, I pray for your happiness" (Psalm 122, 8-9). The leadership of this reconciling agent among men will always be responsive to individual and communal aspirations. The essence of psychotheological worship is to acknowledge this leadership. This kind of authority bridges the gaps between men and shrinks tribal boundaries. The barriers which separate man from the fulfillment of his brotherly aspirations come down in Christ's life. He "made himself God's equal" (John 5, 18), and in so doing enunciated the principles of just leadership and total equality. Thus each man becomes the same, equal with the source of his being.

The role of authority which Christ exerted was childlike in the sense that it held little truck with rigid and fixed rules of conduct in human transactions. Children play their games in the spirit of constant interchange of roles. Dominance and submission are not regarded as exclusive. The players get a chance at all roles sooner or later in the sequence of the game. True leadership is never a constant. The leader seeks in his learner the exalted position of teacher.

An authority, whether clergyman, teacher, therapist or parent, must exercise tenderness. Christ touched men so that they could touch one another. Touching is a great equalizer. The ceremony in which a bishop or priest washes the feet of his people is a symbol of the humility which is to be expected of everyone in authority. This humble attitude has been lacking in the established Church for many centuries. Church officials have taken advantage of the pomp of their offices. Much of this subversion of the role of authority happened because the leaders themselves were living out roles which had been defined in the past. A tremendous breakthrough is needed — a psychotheological approach, warning against stagnant theology. The various transferences and defenses of the ego are operating just as busily in the man of responsibility as in the domineering parent or spouse. In order to reawaken the tender approach, the leaders in Church and government must refine their perceptions. Some period of psychotherapy or counseling for those who occupy the established positions of authority may be one way of reckoning with the temptation to distort the authentic basis of authority.

The man who, like St. Francis of Assisi, can console more than he needs to be consoled and who can understand more than he needs to be understood is well on the way toward making love the essence of his life mission. The emergence of a new breed of leadership will come with self-realization. Each man as his own authority can heed God's call by responding with both eyes to the future. History and experience command each man to participate in life, but leadership must always be based on experience, and never on arrogance.

8

THE SINS OF
AUTHORITY

People today are increasingly alien-
ated from established religion and
politics. Although both Christianity
and democracy proclaim a universal mission, neither demonstrates
much promise for accomplishing it. Ecclesiastical and political
moralists today are more than ever challenged by individuals who
seek experience on their own terms. This is the shape morality
seems to be taking in our day. Many refer to this attitude as "situation ethics," a method of behavior in which most decisions are
made not according to received codes but in accordance with personal needs and ideals. Psychotheology is more inclined to call it
an *ethic of the enigmatic*. It demands a respect for the gap between
personal conduct and rules. What happens in that gap is the mysterious. Even the person who seems to "live by the rules" lives a
life compatible with his experience alone. He is not determined by
his institutions. Rather, his individual experience is noteworthy
both as an end in itself and as a contribution to a society.

Individual and Social Guilt

It is hard to say exactly how society influences a person's moral
sense. But at least we are sure of one thing. Every society which
claims to be democratic and or Christian cannot merely insist on

the duty of its citizens to renew and revitalize the community; it must also safeguard their subtler privilege of being counted as conspirators as well as contributors.

The harmony of a society follows from its willingness to recognize the needs and frustrations of individuals. This means a willingness to allow the individual the right to be treated as more than a ward. When St. Paul wrote that "written letters bring death" (2 Corinthians 3, 6), he knew that every institution has to view individuals ultimately in more than legal terms. The legal mind always attempts to categorize, to regiment individuals into groups or sub-groups. This kind of literalness always tempts the totalitarian mind. A few years ago Americans saw how easily people could be labeled "fifth amendment Communists," "pinkos," or "fellow travelers." The totalitarian impulse in any institution, be it Church or state, tries to impose obeisance to itself. Likewise, the label "law and order" in the mid-20th century usually means that police action, the power of the state, is the only way to insure social survival. This attitude is squarely opposed to the Gospel message of love. Similarly, "peace with honor" often means that national prestige should take precedence over justice and respect for other nations. It is with such self-deceptions that society constricts and distorts morality while morality itself goes by the board.

But no institution can completely subvert Christ's message as long as there are individuals who continue to insist upon their primary obligation to follow his law of universal love. Christ's ideal was spoken of by the prophet Zechariah when he cried out, "He will proclaim peace for the nations. His empire shall stretch from sea to sea, from the River to the ends of the earth" (Zechariah 9, 10). Beautiful as it is, Christ's plan for redemption is constantly threatened with subversion, most often by the institutions that society itself creates.

In a society like ours, beset by violence, war and racism, social harmony can never be imposed. An individual conscience can never move without a corresponding movement on the part of institutions to proclaim themselves publicly guilty. Those who speak most loudly about morality and the need for repentance of the individual often fail to see the necessity of proclaiming their own guilt. The moral sense of any society grows only when it is preceded by an acknowledgment of collective guilt. One cannot exist without the other, any more than personal repentance can exist without a sense of personal guilt.

The two-way street between the institutions and individuals that comprise society affords the channel of communication by which each is reminded of the priority it must give the other. The Church, for example, has to acknowledge its own guilt and not merely judge that of individuals. Only in this way can she claim to speak with any authority about forgiveness. Anything else would smack of totalitarianism and betray the essence of Christ's attitude. Imposition might be the one sin which the Church will have to answer for in the long run. In the past, her idea of authority meant the imposition of legal codes, as if that in itself would guarantee morality. Further, an individual has to be on guard against the temptation to "buy back" the affections of an institution, whether Church or state, for this will succeed only in fostering further fears of what the institution will demand in the future.

Freud cast some light on this latter point when he described "transference," a phenomenon in which earlier experiences are called forth not simply as recollections, but as past events "transferred" to a current relationship. This introduces a host of psychic connections with persons and places that live on in the present. Many such "transferences" are filled with a feeling of happy memories; others reflect the opposite. Thus the present is in some way a reflection of how these experiences, sown in the past, still bear fruit in the here-and-now.

Many transference reactions give rise to continued good relationships, as, for example, with one whose parents were generous toward others, including strangers. Usually children who grow up in such environments have a sense of openness, whereas a child fostered by tense, suspicious, stingy parents will have to battle anxieties when he grows up. He may well see the face of fear even on those close to him. The phenomenon is common, and the resolution of such severe negative transference may even require special professional help. The Church, whose history is strewn with such limiting parental visions, thus might herself be responsible for present moral limitations against groups of individuals such as the blacks, the poor and the "socially unacceptable."

The ideal transference resolution is discovered in a moral and psychic attitude which sees a right to uniqueness in others. From a psychotheological point of view, to say each man is Christ may serve to remind us that prejudice and hatred are, in reality, types of unresolved transference and that only through great psychospiritual efforts can one hope to understand the universal moral vision of Christ himself. This can never be an impersonal search. People look for intimacy and love, and in order to find them other persons must be present. One cannot work out the limiting influences of negative transference outside of personal relationships. That is why even the most acute problems of society can be worked out in a personal context. Although it is helpful to see love in cosmic terms, no universal moral sense was ever developed outside of personal experiences. To the extent that society, the Church, and the state have not helped persons to accomplish this, they have failed in their redemptive mission.

To call upon a man to contribute to the common need is to ask him to broaden his vision. The pursuit of universal morality to which all men are called is always beset by resistances. People have a difficult time appraising each other's experiences. Cultural biases and prejudices prevent the free and open acknowledgment of differences. All of us as infants are initially bound by an unreal omnipotence that is superseded eventually by more rational attitudes as we mature. Yet people who fear a loss of prestige often fail to let go of this infantile sense of omnipotence as it affects relations with "strangers." What must be substituted is a kind of self-appraisal which, from a psychotheological standpoint, stands as its own reward, in that it overcomes infantilism by grasping at a large moral vision.

Again Christ is the relevant symbol here. His power, according to St. Paul, is felt "in the heavens, on earth and in the underworld" (Philippians 2, 10). But it is ironic that often, in order for Christ's relevance to be felt, men have to break the chains that institutional morality impose on their experience. Moral and psychological values are the only links that bind men together, and whoever fails to see the human race in such terms has failed to recognize what Christ himself wanted.

The Guilt of the Church

Like the prophet, an individual suffering from moral and psychological wounds cries out, "These I received in the house of my friends" (Zechariah 13, 6). Such cries of anguish have often been directed at the Church as an institution, at her laws coldly administered, and at her indifference to the suffering and hardship endured by those trying to obey those laws.

The Church must acknowledge that she has failed all too often to share the anxieties of the individual heart. Men today scorn the Church for these reasons, and their accusations read like a perverted litany: They curse her for her refusal to come to terms with the most relevant factors of human experience, for being a tool of the rich when Christ preached personal poverty, for supporting war when Christ gave his life for peace, for condoning white supremacy, whether tacitly or overtly, when Christ preached the sacredness of each individual.

Each time these charges are made, they point to the reality of the collective guilt of the Christian Church. The Church has too often been an unwilling penitent bound by the same security device used by compulsive neurotics. Although such accusations are painful to hear, they are periodically necessary and healthy. If the individual does not remind the Church (or any other institution which claims to safeguard morality), how else will she be cleansed and renewed? Only thus can accumulated and collective resistances, which often pass for tradition, be exposed, freeing the institution to work for mankind's future. That the Lord "punishes all those that he acknowledges as his sons" (Hebrews 12, 6) is as true for the Church as for any individual.

Psychotheology insists that it is wrong from both a psychological and a religious viewpoint to speak of guilt without illuminating the social context of blame. All action is synergistic with each person reflecting and responding automatically to his environment. When a man confesses his sins, he is in part revealing those actions to which the Church herself has had a hand in exposing him because she has accepted society's immorality. No one person can ever be asked to bear the whole burden of any evil act. The Church has too long viewed the penitent as a man on his knees asking forgiveness. He is rather an individual in relationship to society, whether a member of an oppressed group or even the oppressor himself.

Perhaps the reason why traditional Church moralists have had so little to say about the importance of social morality is that they have understood so little of social forces. Psychologists suggest that anti-social behavior is an outgrowth of loneliness and tension. True forgiveness, then, should flow from the belief that we have each made life a series of misunderstandings. When a man does wrong to others, he is at least signaling his hope that they may recognize something in him which even he has failed to note. Destructive behavior dates back to the moments early in life where one has been denied the warmth of total acceptance. Brotherhood, or what the Church calls fraternal charity, is meant to seal this gap.

Forgiveness must be exercised in all human experience. The Church herself has to seek forgiveness for her failure to understand the strivings of those whom she proclaims as sinners. Without such an attitude, there can hardly be any lasting or meaningful absolution for society at large.

The breakdown of morale in any society — and we in America have experienced this quite dramatically in recent years — can never be explained away by attributing it merely to individuals, or even to groups of individuals. Like the psychologist who specializes in group dynamics, the Church must be honest enough to expose hidden hostilities even in the so-called "leaders" of society — family, government, the Church herself. Such groups may themselves be subject to infantile fears which, when not uprooted, tend to subvert society's ideals. In a psychotheological sense, society can come to grips with its own self-destructive tendencies only when moral ideals are preached in terms of psychological honesty and not merely mouthed by professional pietists.

Like all ideals which are meant to strengthen unity, Christ's kingdom of love on earth is constantly being resisted and subverted. Resistance to social unity is no different from psychic resistance to individual wholeness. People remain at war with themselves, and this veil hides a person's eyes from his full potentials. He often employs it in order to "protect" himself from his responsibilities. There would be no reason for psychological defenses if human beings felt able to respond to what they know of themselves.

Sometimes the Church has the power to discourage morality. There are people who feel close to her but who are appalled by her alliances with governments of privileged groups. Some persons who wish to change their values meet resistance within their families, their government or Church. And so those who might otherwise grow in maturity refrain from doing so in order not to be "excommunicated" psychologically.

The two individuals who were crucified beside Christ on Calvary shared his fate in the sense that they, too, were not understood by the moralists of their day. They were destroyed by a society that could, but would not, listen. The criminal of any society is symbolic — he dies as the man misunderstood by his time but nonetheless ready to remind institutionalized morality how really removed it can be from the ordinary needs of man.

Everyone can find psychological fulfillment in Christ's vision of morality. When we say that he redeemed mankind, we mean that he gave human experience the power to try to become more than itself. Our blindness to each other is reflected in society at large. As people are allowed to trample on each other's aspirations, they likewise extinguish Christ's vision of a society which would constantly renew itself while preparing itself for religious and psychological fulfillment.

Resistances to Christ's plan are not easily overcome, least of all by institutions. The fear of losing prestige has frequently become the concern of nations which fall into totalitarianism. But for the Church there can never be anything intrinsically bad in admitting her own weakness and stupidity. The Christian message, in spite of everything, in spite of even what the Church herself has done to subvert it, triumphs only when it places love above force, humility before ambition. It is only when the Church uses her authority to preserve her stability that she runs the risk, as she has in the past, of losing her very soul.

It is only recently that people have come to see that their need for morality involves more than the need for stability or the desire for security with which some religious leaders tempt them. They have come to realize that their very freedom is threatened in the subtlest ways, sometimes by those who claim to protect it. Nowhere are we reminded of this more forcefully than in the voices of those who once were slaves.

It is strange that psychological and moral slavery exist in a nation which calls itself Christian and democratic. But the mystery may be partly explained by the fact that the Church has allowed her people to rely heavily on political slogans to achieve social morality. A society which builds its moral sense on political expediency without acceptance of moral principles allows the political mind to dominate its morality. It invites social immorality, violence and disaster.

Saints understand this. They have always seen that possessive slavery is immoral and not merely socially or politically unacceptable. For them freedom is a moral imperative, not a political slogan. They suffer because they live in societies which do not listen to this message. But true martyrs are always morally and psychologically sound; their suffering is sacramental; moral principles are psychologically compelling for them; the fact that others do not see this sharpens their agony and reaffirms their commitment.

Even the healthy instinct to suffer for the good of society can be abused and taken advantage of. It is easy to prescribe suffering for the wrong reasons. The Church has insisted upon suffering without at times realizing its full psychological implications. It is easy to believe that the only way to salvation is through pain, but if this becomes the only means of deliverance then suffering loses its purpose; it becomes a self-imposed torment motivated by a selfish desire to rid oneself of all "personal imperfection." Obviously, it is not difficult to set up moral and political codes geared to satisfy instincts. The end result is that we have cults in which the holy man, even Christ himself, becomes idealized simply because of the torment he has borne. People in authority are easily tempted to make suffering a basic value. Psychotheologically speaking, however, the value of self-inflicted sacrifice is hard to understand unless the individual is motivated to work for the betterment of the world at large. When psychologically abused, an emphasis on suffering and self-sacrifice can reinforce man's instinct to destroy — himself as well as others.

We are coming to realize that the racial tyranny laid upon the black man has often been justified by white society's belief that suffering is the black man's lot. He was meant to bear the white man's burden, to sit humbly at the back of the wedding feast, or to hang from the cross. Today, many whites are shocked by the black rebellion, as if blacks were somehow failing their penitential mission.

The perversion that results from this kind of social immorality is even more shocking when we consider how many oppressed people in the past wallowed in their slavery. They chose subordination and humiliation precisely for the reassurance of living within a circumscribed world. Psychologically they gave up hope of being understood and they settled for a life of subjugation. The prototypical "Uncle Tom" who fawned before his oppressors found that even his speech and his seeming dull-wittedness were incorporated into society's vision of him. By then it was too late to reform society; its wellsprings had become poisoned. That is why for many blacks today a psychic as well as a moral and political revolution seems imperative.

It is no accident that many contemporary black militants are throwing over institutional morality. Many have even renounced Christianity and are taking their stand against psychological, moral and economic subjugation. They repudiate white society, including the white man's word for them — "Negro." Some have adopted a violent rhetoric because heretofore all personal expression has been denied them. Even external violence is part of the black man's refusal to accept the stereotype that the white man imposed on him for centuries.

It may be true that black men were foolish to adopt a religion whose practitioners were responsible for enslaving them. But black men have given the Christian Gospel its first real moral and psychological challenge from within, and are thus renewing the very morality that white Christians think they have renounced. If today the black man is reliving the exodus, it is not because he is "special," but because he has, in the face of suffering, kept faith in his own future. He is looking for a promised land where religious values will be based on psychological health.

Youth and the Power Structure

Today we are told that the gap between generations is wider than it has ever been, since youth is not only rejecting traditional values but seeing experience in a radically new light. One can "drop out" in many ways: drugs, alcohol, religion, films, philosophy. But whatever element is employed, they say, it is a vehicle for encounter with self and one's relationships, the means by which one can unfold potentialities for expansion.

Adolescence as a recognized social institution is a recent phenomenon. Not until recently was it acknowledged as an interest group in its own right. The teens and the early twenties have long been regarded merely as stepping-stones to maturity. Now the image of the awkward teenager has given way to the image of the social critic. Youth is striving to join forces with the electric and post-industrial revolution. The typical young man spoofs the logic of a generation which he considers imprisoned by its own rationalism. His very thinking is non-linear; it defies traditional moral and psychological rules.

Many persons believe that today's young man is hedonistic and uncommitted, and they maintain that his experience is not to be trusted. But perhaps the suspicions that adult society has of such attitudes reflect its own psychological and moral shortsightedness. In plain fact, the adolescent may be creating a real charismatic community of his own. Be-ins, happenings, soul music, light shows, peace marches, civil protests — these may be indications of a new liturgy in which moral and psychological values are finding à convergent expression. They may be pointing to a valid and genuinely new psychotheological experience for which the power structure is not prepared.

Society is correct in reminding young people that the results of experimentation are neither predictably good nor predictably bad. Anyone may be fooled into thinking he is charismatic. Nonconformism does not relieve anyone of the need to choose between development and retardation, between active search and selfish gratification. Aspirations may result in rapture or terror, in sanctity or degeneracy. But youth always reminds us that the risk is worth taking. One may meet the undiscovered self, as Jacob did when he wrestled with the angel. Though crippled, he would not yield without a blessing: "Your name shall no longer be Jacob, but Israel," the angel said; "because you have been strong against God, you shall prevail against men" (Genesis 32, 28-30).

Like any leap into maturity, Jacob's change of name represented a new, more firmly committed identity. To be sure, Israel had been defined before his struggle with the angel; as Jacob, he had even tricked his father into giving him the birthright that belonged to Esau, his elder brother, the symbol of stability. Jacob symbolized the man who took a chance, who broke with conventional morality, who confronted the challenge of creating meaning out of struggle. As youth instinctively knows, this is the only sure path to authenticity. Each generation faces a new age of consciousness and new, undreamed potentialities of the human mind. Every age reaches the dawn of its own yearnings. The question the establishment has to ask itself is whether or not it will allow youth to move on to full responsibility in and for the social structure. Will youth achieve, for its own purposes, a clearer understanding of the unconscious? Will it be able to make moral sense out of moral chaos? As psychotheology sees it, only by answering these questions will society be able to answer the needs of its youth and prevent itself from falling into the faults it has perpetrated in the past.

In youth's "dropping out" we see the odyssey of an emerging society. Putting oneself out of conventional controls is youth's way today of forcing its own limb out of joint, as Jacob's hip was dislocated while he wrestled. Jacob was not permitted to know the name of the divine being with whom he struggled; neither has the chaos of modern society any name to offer youth. Yet chaos permits new meanings to be wrested from it. It is youth's prerogative to choose by active seizure of the new. Such a seizing is engagement, and in our time engagement is the only liberating factor. Youth has taught society that much. There is no room for moral indifference on the part of a significant number of the young.

Youth has good reason to question the motives of a society which claims to furnish all necessary advantages. To hold a young person by the scruff of the neck from a thirty-story building and protest that because we love him we will not let him drop hardly indicates authentic concern. On the other hand, the relaxation of irrational restrictiveness and the attempt to arrive at some understanding of the concerns which seem to obsess many of today's young people require a real and honest reassessment of our limited moral and psychological vision. Today words like "coddling," "pampering" and "indulging" are shibboleths. The young are no longer bound by the morality and psychology of the past. When adult society insists on applying outworn psychomoral concepts, youth has good reason to feel threatened.

Some ways of motivating young people to enter the ranks of society are lacking in moral and psychological honesty. "A few years in the army will make a man of you" and "When you finally get your hair cut then we'll see about giving you a job" are typical examples of dishonesty employed to initiate the young. These types of societal baptism are a frequent weapon of a group with economic power. They are attempts to get a young person to "mend his ways" and begin behaving as if his mission in life could never be authentic. They rarely acknowledge the positive values that the present generation of youth seeks. Once again the Church and society will cry out that they have lost the young. But today it will be true, for they will have failed to allow new psychological understanding the room it needs to give sharper focus to moral values.

For the younger generation, certain moral taboos of the past are no longer meaningful. The very word "heresy" has become meaningless. Spiritual experimentation is a characteristic of our time. That is why the psychotheological emphasis seems so pertinent, for a psychotheological view gives first place to those forces which guide the emerging personality. It even assents to moral and political "rebellion," which may in reality be a shift in perspective, the awakening of a new religious sensibility. Not even all the so-called destructive behavior of youthful agitators can be called retrogressive. Their desire to resist conformity may mean that they are attempting to bury traditions which the older generation recognizes as dead but is unwilling to change. Thus young people protect themselves from the rot of tradition. And they do this even at the risk of paying the high price of remaining part of society.

But where and how, society has a right to ask, will the rebellion end? With psychoanalysis? With religious renewal? The new generation will have to call upon whatever psychic and moral values it can muster, wherever it can find them in experience. As the author of the book of Revelation says: "I saw a new heaven and a new earth; the first heaven and the first earth had disappeared" (Revelation 21, 1). For tomorrow's world, the altered structure of experience will assume new shapes. Like a surrealist composition, the new shape will be no less organized than the shape it superseded, but it will have been regenerated; creation will have occurred once more, mystery once more revealed. The new heaven of the future is always an adventure, as the New Earth is.

The new generation sees a future which the older is not prepared to see. Today it speaks to objects and machines, as well as to people, with the love and comprehension with which St. Francis spoke to Brother Wolf and Sister Sun. In so doing, it asserts its own moral and psychological prerogatives and breaks free from a society which would prevent it from experiencing life in its own way.

This new age can produce a deeper spiritual sense based on psychological insight and honesty and dedicated to avoiding the errors of the past. Its moral and psychological powers will be dedicated to achieving a new role for the individual in society, based on the sacredness of all human relationships. Out of such relationships, visibly and pragmatically experienced, can come a love that is characterized by acceptance and not by mere acquiescence, a love that is based on an appreciation of the uniqueness of each person, a love that will give a new moral dimension to society itself.

But this entails a deeper, a more psychological, understanding of the Power we call God and how he moves among men. Only thus will youth be able to see what those before them sought but could not find. And they will have moved at least a little closer to a fuller realization of Christ's influence on earth.

POSTSCRIPT

A spirit of convergence pervades man's quest for knowledge, and yet each of us tends to look at things from the viewpoint of his own experience. So does psychotheology. From our vantage point, man's search for insights into his world is sacred; it is a way to relating with God and the world. As we have tried to show, psychotheology asserts that a man's experience is all-important. Outside his experience, myths, moral teachings, and devotions carry little psychological weight. Man is wed to a larger community, and he achieves cosmic significance insofar as he allows his consciousness to develop on all levels. It is essential to both therapeutic psychology and religious devotion that man become more alive to himself and more open to his experiences. He relates to the things around him in order to affirm his own life and give witness to the glory of creation. Each person achieves this in ways that transcend explicit definition. Asked by the Pharisees when the kingdom of God was to come, Jesus answered: "The coming of the kingdom of God does not admit of observation, and there will be no one to say 'Look here! Look there!' For, you must know, the kingdom of God is among you" (Luke 17, 20-21).

The unity of experience that a person feels as he comes to know more of himself is the ultimate goal of the religious and the psychological journey. A person becomes more involved as he opens more of himself to himself. Psychoanalysis, for instance, tries to replace the unconscious with consciousness. The Gospels use the word "light" for both Christ and knowledge. "All that came to be had life in him, and that life was the light of men, a light that shines in the dark, a light that darkness could not overpower" (John 1, 4-5). For a Christian, Jesus is "the light of the world" (John 8, 12), and by this illumination he is freed from "the domination of Satan" and is given "a share in the inheritance of the sanctified" (Acts 26, 18) — what we would call in psychotheological terms "religious maturity" and "psychological integration."

Psychotheology maintains that the convergence of the theological and psychological journeys is more than a possibility — it is a fact. It is consistent with the times, for it acknowledges the many avenues of convergence being taken by modern man in order to discover his potentialities. It can discern — especially in emerging groups such as the blacks and youth — the thrust of human consciousness trying to make itself felt. The new forms of expression these groups are using are a further transformation of the human race, bringing light where there once was darkness.

A convergent approach to life such as ours speaks to man in his own language. The recitation of a creed for its own sake has no place in the contemporary vocabulary if it does not reflect what is actually experienced. Either the commandments, beatitudes and healings of the Old and New Testaments have immediate relevance in a person's perception of the world or they have no relevance for him at all. As a person grows he may become increasingly conscious of a particular spiritual insight, but unless he is "at one" with what is proclaimed, it does not exist for him. Likewise, no psychological principle has any worth in a person's life if it does not have immediate impact on his experience. All the guidance in the world — religious or psychological — will produce little more than intellectualization unless it verifies genuine experience.

The journey of modern man must be based upon the primacy of personal truth and the liberating value of reality. And these must be expressed in his movements toward others rather than in set formulas. Genuine religion denies labels. It is not enough for a man to espouse a given set of doctrines; it is not enough for him to speak of the future as if he fully understands what he means. Labels and creeds are idols for a psychologically sophisticated person. He keeps faith with his world to the extent that he validates his life by fending off resistances to openness. Everyone experiences resistances — fragments of the past which distort the future. People overlay the present with memories and personalities of the past, making their present stance shaky. There is a universal tendency to hold on to the forces of reaction, for the urge to progressive social and political movement is fraught with the fear of what is new and uncertain. People hold on to the past no matter how painful it has been for them. At least they survived the past; no matter how unpleasant or ugly it was, they came out of it alive.

Yet to be alive *is* to journey. Psychotheology borrows freely from psychoanalytic psychology to reveal the resistances and transferences carried over from the past. It accepts the religious belief that man has a destiny which is realizable, if not always fully available. Man is engaged in a process that allows him to acknowledge inner tensions and to face them with enlightenment. All experience must constantly be renewed. Death is an ever present reality; so is the impermanence of material possession. Yet the experience of permanence is both a hope and a valid belief that, despite loss, the essential quality of the journey remains. Were it not for this permanence there would be no hope at all. Isaiah 51, 6 says:

> Lift up your eyes to the heavens,
> look down at the earth.
> The heavens will vanish like smoke.
> the earth wear out like a garment,
> and its inhabitants die like vermin;
> But my salvation shall last forever
> and my justice have no end.

Psychotheology considers how man relates to this concept of the enduring and the eternal. If eternity becomes merely an excuse for enduring, then it is not authentic for a man to live in a non-static universe. If, on the other hand, the dynamic and progressive aspects of life are acknowledged, then uncertainty itself becomes a viable form of hope and faith. Joy can be manifested in the knowledge that there is always renewal, that infinity is constant. As God so beautifully says in the *Bhagavad Gita,* "There is no end to my divine manifestations." Psychotheology accepts man as a person involved in process, securing his sanity each day as he relates to the principle of uncertainty, to his God, in the healthiest ways available to him.

Uncertainty can be exciting. Modern men no longer expect their religion, government, or other social institutions to provide them with all the answers. Social importance is found in each individual life, and it is discovered when people remain personally and culturally open. Modern religious sensibility is aware of this, and yet the conditioning of the past pressures people to resist it. They try to influence the direction of the future by patterning their lives on the "safety" of the past.

Old Testament stories in which God seeks out man are important in the psychotheological appreciation of the human condition. They mirror the truism that experience is the pivot of life. Divine consciousness might be called Supreme Experience. God comes alive through his creation, especially as man becomes more conscious of himself. The forces of reaction try to crush the spirit by forcing God into a cubbyhole. Ezekiel said, "Hear the word of Yahweh. The Lord Yahweh says this: Woe to the foolish prophets who follow their own spirit, without seeing anything" (Ezekiel 13, 1-3).

The insights of psychoanalytic psychology make it increasingly possible for us to recognize the immorality of prejudice and reaction. A therapist can study how transference and resistance affect free behavior. It no longer seems reasonable to exempt theological dogmas from the experiential inquiry available through the psychoanalytic disciplines.

A man's future depends upon his constant alertness to the events and experiences of his life. The sacred will be located where consciousness is allowed to grow. Christ is not some mysterious or ambiguous merger of man and God; he is God fully alive as man, and vice versa. And this universal wedding of all life is further specified in each person. Jesus is man coming to a full awareness of who he is.

Throughout the ages, Christianity has sought to collect mankind's experiences, giving them a frame of reference and sanctifying their relevance in terms of human redemption. This allows the ministry of the Word to announce a creation that is not static but unfolding. Psychotheology further identifies creation with the continual emergence of consciousness: the Word becomes the enlargement of the ego, and consequently the presence of social awareness. Even the sacramental life of the Church celebrates the creative principle in history. The Church continually anoints mankind, proclaiming to men "a new birth as [God's] sons" (1 Peter 1, 3). The Easter mystery marks the rebirth of the people of God and the distribution of the real essence of life to those who would receive it. Every man shares in the ministries of Christ. The Church of the future will have to see herself as truly universal, as the authentic collection of mankind's hopes and aspirations.

Our spiritual and psychological heritages are articulated in our ability to respond to the demands of creation. There are times, however, when conflicts of interest are unavoidable. When this happens, people become confused, perhaps forgetting their responsibility for their relationships to themselves and others. Their vision is blurred; it grabs hold of any security. This predicament is accompanied by a feeling of being apart from the rest of men. A person feels unwanted and unloved; he has, as it were, excommunicated himself through a sense of unworthiness. The inability to respond to the demands of life is referred to by religious thinkers as a "loss of faith" or "crisis of faith" and by psychological practitioners as disassociation and alienation. Psychotheology, while not a system of psychotherapy, would describe this existential predicament as the moment between death and rebirth, the sacramental moment when an important creative happening is about to occur. Thus the solace of religion and the sympathy of the psychotherapist may serve to emphasize the implications of this "fall from grace."

The true Church of the future, not excluding any experience, must stand ready to welcome the disturbed, the troubled and the frightened. Every man, in a psychotheological sense, stands ready to experience creation. The Church's exercise of authority will have to be more than judgmental. It must be open, providing an index of reality and responsibility. In order to understand good and evil, truth and error, pleasure and pain, adventure and stagnation, it is important for people to have a core of wisdom to which they may turn. Obviously, this core cannot be rigid, it must be progressive, helping an individual to stand on the frontier of his time. Reality and responsibility become visible when individuals are prepared to accept their sensibilities and desires. They must be assured that to be alive is good, that they themselves are worthwhile. In short, psychotheology sees the Church of the future as representing a Christ who is the universal root of all experience.

Each individual shares in the flux of creation. The process of social evolution breaks down barriers between individuals, but it cannot proceed without the full cooperation of the individual person. Our belief that human motivation is the source of worship can be justified by acknowledging that motivation must be open to the future. Psychotheology has defined God as the future, because the destiny of mankind rests upon a full acceptance of the many tomorrows which in some form are already at hand.

Each man is an embodiment of how creation will express itself. The collective unconscious which is part of each person's identity includes not only the past history of all life, but also the potentialities available to those who keep faith with the basic dignity of the human experience. In this sense, psychotheology bridges the gap between the human and the divine. Life is of a piece as is creation. God is the dynamic unifier who draws his creation into harmony. The ideal of the peacemaker is always sacred, since peace reduces discord and antagonism.

St. Paul says that God "has taken us out of the power of darkness and created a place for us in the kingdom of the Son that he loves, and in him we gain our freedom" (Colossians 1, 13-14), and that "in his [Christ's] body lives the fullness of divinity, and in him you too find your own fulfillment" (Colossians 2, 9). The peacemaking task is the acknowledgment of a "fullness" in which each element corresponds to all others. Likewise, the psychoanalytic task is to bring unconscious drives to a point of harmony with the conscious ones — to bring conflicting personality aspects into unison. In the Christian sense, true freedom waits on this "fullness." For psychotheology, Christ is the world reconciled.

This vision of life does not contradict the hope of mankind. Each person retains his own integrity and character for Christ's sense of universality is not totalitarian. Psychotheology is alert to the dynamic of life: everything which has being corresponds; no one part commands. Even in an individual person, each element of the psyche responds to every other element. This unifying principle is called *wholistic* by psychologists. Nothing can exist outside of relationships, even though no two personality factors are alike.

So it is in the social sphere where love and understanding are based upon communication and dialogue. Once a man is understood he is no danger. It is wrong to assume that understanding requires no effort. Stereotyping, which is easy, guarantees animosity and hatred. Each strange nation or person remains a parish in the eyes of a man who refuses to open his eyes to the unity of creation.

Prayer is communication between man and God — the future dimension — and between man and man — the present. In a true socio-religious sense, prayer also links us with the past. As Christ said to those who would listen: "Do not imagine that I have come to abolish the Law or the Prophets. I have not come to abolish but to complete them" (Matthew 5, 17). The religion of the future will see more clearly that nothing beautiful or real in the experience of mankind can be ignored. Christian social conscience can become more authentic by recognizing the past as a motivating factor toward unity. The past is not sacred in and of itself. This misunderstanding of heritage leads to dissension and prejudice. The past need not be protected; it must, rather, be enlisted as the motivation for progress.

Moral power in the human experience comes into play as mankind partakes of many unions — people with people, past with future, church with church, individuality with collectivity. The resulting convergence is what creation itself symbolizes. In the psychotheological sense, Christ can "happen" only as men learn to "worship each other." The effort which must be expended is enormous. People must first learn who they are. This self-seeking requires all the psychotherapeutic and religious forces available. In addition it requires a responsiveness to the directions being marked out in the art forms, since it is the artist who seeks an expression of life that is more significantly comprehensible than it has ever been in the past. The behavioral and social sciences act as the yeast in raising man's potential as a relating being. Sociology, anthropology, medicine, biology, urban planning, will all lend their genius to the betterment of mankind.

The physical sciences define and enhance our environment. Life must always have an evolving atmosphere in which to expand. Mankind is impatient for a unified view of life and the universe. This was as much Einstein's hope as it was Newton's, or Spinoza's, or Teilhard's. Nevertheless, matter and man's relationship to it are always in flux. For psychotheology, nourished by psychological and spiritual inquiry, life is a process, and the process is sacred. Nothing so dynamic can ever be fixed. It proceeds in the direction of its own best expression, the Omega of Teilhard or the heaven of the New Covenant. This convergence is truly personal, since it involves full participation of each living being. No science, no religion, can survive without an expansion of self-knowledge. This knowledge must help each individual to free himself from a neurotic dependence which may express itself in a multitude of prejudices and rigidities.

The future will bring new means of helping men locate their feelings. But it may also bring the means with which humanity can end its place in the universe. The choice is between the kind of self-disclosure which serves to place one in relationship with life, and the self-deceit which locks the doors to the true hope of convergence. Thus, for psychotheology, self-knowledge is more than a penetration of motives. It is the opening of the eye, which past evil experiences may have closed, to the appreciation of the fullness and sacredness of life. Psychotheology speaks to the future. It reminds 20th-century man that to be human is to be sacred, that it is only through self-understanding that man can learn to see how truly he is the image of his God.